"Throughout my business and expedition career I have faced many challenging situations. Learning to deal with stress is a key part of navigating a busy life. I used to believe that mentally tough people were 'special' but have learned that they are not. They were not born with natural mental toughness or inner resilience – they developed it over years. This required them to improve their emotional control by working with tools and processes to enhance resilience and strengthen determination. They learned to accept that temporary setbacks will always happen and need to be dealt with. In this book Penny identifies the critical tools and processes needed to develop the resilience and mental toughness needed to carry on and be successful regardless of what the world throws at you. Read it and thrive!"

Kevin Gaskell, Business Leader, Author, Adventurer

365 WAYS TO DEVELOP MENTAL TOUGHNESS

365 WAYS
TO DEVELOP MENTAL TOUGHNESS

BY PENNY MALLORY

First published in Great Britain by John Murray Learning in 2022
An imprint of John Murray Press
A division of Hodder & Stoughton Ltd,
An Hachette UK company

1

A CIP catalogue record for this title is available from the British Library

Hardback ISBN 978 1 52939 764 2
eBook ISBN 978 1 52939 763 5

Typeset by KnowledgeWorks Global Ltd.

Printed and bound in Great Britain by Clays Ltd, Elcograf S.p.A.

John Murray Press policy is to use papers that are natural, renewable and
recyclable products and made from wood grown in sustainable forests.
The logging and manufacturing processes are expected to conform to the
environmental regulations of the country of origin.

John Murray Press
Carmelite House
50 Victoria Embankment
London EC4Y 0DZ

www.johnmurraypress.co.uk

CONTENTS

ABOUT THE AUTHOR

Despite a relatively privileged start to life, Penny was an unhappy child. Her mother suffered very severely from manic-depression (or bipolar as its now known), drank heavily and chain smoked. She loved her father but was secretly scared of him. Her growing up years were confusing and unhappy.

As a child, Penny admits she was average at everything, and excelled at nothing. At age seven, being awarded for 'Endeavour' just about summed her up. It was her first experience of being celebrated for being 'average'.

Penny didn't fit in at school, or feel comfortable anywhere, even at home. Like many other teenagers, she sought attention by misbehaving, which, in its own way, was her inner strength and independence starting to form. As her schoolwork and attitude deteriorated, she ran away (aged 14) and never returned home. She lost touch with her father for the next 20 years.

Eventually, Penny lost control of her life and hit rock bottom. She stayed in homeless hostels, and sofa-surfed for several years. At her lowest point, she decided to borrow some money and have a go at her lifelong dream of driving rally cars. That first day at a rally school offered Penny an environment where she felt 'at home' for the first time.

Being around world class performers inspired her to excel and develop her mental toughness so she could succeed and win. She became obsessed with human performance because she desperately wanted to understand: 'what makes a winner?'

After 12 years of working tirelessly to drive rally cars, against all the odds, she became the first and only woman in the world to drive for Ford in the World Rally Championship.

Penny went on to present many car programmes on television, train as a performance coach and become a leading authority on mental toughness as well as a master practitioner in cognitive behavioural therapy (CBT). She has climbed two of the world's Seven Summits, fought in two boxing fights, run multiple marathons, and written three books on human performance.

Penny is a highly acclaimed international keynote speaker on mental toughness, and this book brings together 365 ways you too can develop your mental toughness.

INTRODUCTION

Take any person on the planet who has achieved success of any kind and you will see that they have mental toughness. It doesn't matter whether they are athletes, scientists, entrepreneurs, politicians or parents, the fact is that anyone who has excelled at anything is mentally tough.

Achieving success is not easy. No one evades the minefield of setbacks, crisis, tragedy and challenge that is part of being alive. Life throws obstacles in your path daily, but your state of mind is the difference that can ensure your success.

Mentally tough people can manage the stress and pressure of life. They see challenges as opportunities. They persist no matter what. They pick themselves up and go again. They are confident, humble, feel in control and are 100 per cent committed to what they set out to achieve.

This may sound like mentally tough people are 'special'. They are not. They were not born with mental toughness – they developed it over years, by deliberately practising and working on their resilience, determination, emotional control and focus… and you can do that, too. If you can manage the stress and pressure you face, you are more likely to live a happy, enjoyable and successful life. If you crumble under the strain of it all, then you will enjoy less fun, happiness and health.

This book is designed to give you a new idea every day, to help you develop your mental toughness. Practise them regularly and see the difference it makes. Keep applying them and you will be developing your mental toughness every single day. You will see that some tips are similar to others but with slight variations, and this is done purposefully to help you embrace and embed valuable concepts, ideas, themes and tasks.

And today is the very best day to start making those positive changes!

CHAPTER 1

WHAT'S YOUR WHY?

1   The story of the wolf and the crane

A wolf had a bone stuck in his throat. He hired a crane, for a large sum of money, to put her head in his throat and remove the bone. When the crane removed the bone, she demanded her reward. The wolf smiled and replied, 'Surely you've been given enough reward by me not eating you?'

The Lesson: Don't expect a reward when serving the wicked. If you help someone, do it out of the kindness of your heart and if you are not rewarded for your good deeds, be grateful that your situation isn't worse. It's selfish to think you'll be rewarded in all situations for kindness. Sometimes it's about building a positive relationship with that person and not about the reward.

2   Zoom out

Maintaining a healthy outlook can be hard, so keep your challenges and troubles in perspective without losing sight of what you need to accomplish. Zoom out. Pull back, slow down and recalibrate. Today, remind yourself of what is going well and what learning you can take from the situation you find yourself in.

Focus on the bigger picture and your longer-term goals. Understand what is really important to you and try not to let the small things dominate your thinking. Focus on what matters. Remember that everybody has good and bad days, and we all have to deal with unexpected events and changes in our life.

Accepting that temporary setbacks happen makes them easier to deal with. As you build your mental toughness, you'll be able to carry on regardless of what the world seems to throw at you.

3   Your own happy

No one is in control of your happiness but you. No one can 'make' you feel anything. Happy or sad, angry or peaceful – *you* are in charge of every emotion you feel, and therefore *you* have the power to change anything about yourself, or your life, that you want to change.

Write down what makes you happy and what your happy life would look like. If you can't articulate this, then you will never be completely clear how to achieve it. If you can define it exactly, no amount of influence from others will touch you.

The happiness you seek has to be based on your version of happiness and not someone else's. Never compare your happiness to that of anyone on TV or social media, or that of friends and colleagues.

4   Find your why

Why do you get up every day? What's the point of your life? When you understand your reason/purpose/mission/goal/why (call it what you will), you'll be more capable of pursuing the things that give you fulfilment. It will serve as your point of reference for all your actions and decisions from this moment on, allowing you to measure your progress and know when you have met your goals. Having a clear sense of purpose, a sense of control, and a feeling that your life is worthwhile is critical to your happiness and quality of life. It may even extend your life expectancy. What's your why?

5   Your natural high

When you smile, your brain releases tiny molecules called neuropeptides, to help fight off stress. Keep smiling and other neurotransmitters like dopamine, serotonin and endorphins come into play, too. The endorphins act as a mild pain reliever and the serotonin is an antidepressant. Together, these brain chemicals make you feel good from head to toe. Not only do they elevate your mood, they also relax your body, reduce physical pain, reduce blood pressure and build endurance.

Smiling is a natural drug you can take daily, in any sized dose – I'm sure you've seen studies showing that smiling a lot will even make you live a longer, happier life.

6   Find your motivation

Today we are going to be doing an exercise to discover what motivates you.

First, write down three things that inspire you to take action. Perhaps it's learning a new skill or listening to a certain type of music, or you might feel especially motivated when you spend time with like-minded people.

Now, write down three things that cause your motivation to evaporate. It could include eating sugary food, catering to your perfectionist tendencies or spending time with pessimistic people.

This exercise will reveal environmental influences on your emotions and your motivation. Once you're aware of them, you can make sensible adjustments that better serve your longer-term goals.

7   Your iceberg mind

Your mind is like an iceberg – it floats with only one-seventh of its bulk above water.

Your conscious mind is exposed to the surface and contains all the thoughts, memories, feelings and wishes that reflect where you are at any given moment. Then there's your subconscious (or unconscious) mind: that vast reservoir of feelings, thoughts, urges and memories that are outside your conscious awareness. It is immensely powerful and runs your life because it stores your beliefs, experiences, memories and skills.

You are in charge of your mind, so start to determine whether the information you have stored is helpful or hurtful and become aware of how it affects your performance. Consciously let go of unhelpful and outdated negative beliefs ('I can't do this', 'I'm no good at that') and replace them with ideas and beliefs that work for you today.

8   Your gut has the answer

Your gut instinct, or intuition, is your immediate understanding of something. When you trust your gut, there's no need to think it over or get another opinion, you just know.

When your gut feeling is at play, you feel a certain kind of clarity about what's going on. Trusting your intuition is the ultimate act of trusting yourself. Importantly, listening to your intuition helps you avoid unhealthy relationships and situations. So, listen to your gut, your intuition, your immediate thought or feeling. Lean in, and trust yourself.

You know much more than you give yourself credit for.

9   Your favourite teacher

According to Carl Jung, the psychoanalyst, as humans we can aim for excellence but perfection remains the realm of the gods.

Perfectionism is irrational thinking. There is no way you can do everything perfectly. When you take a perfectionist viewpoint, you're more likely to procrastinate and achieve less because it's hard to start something when you carry the belief that you won't be successful.

To beat perfectionism you need to change your thoughts about being perfect. Reframe your thinking by accepting that success has its ups and downs. You can't have a great outcome every time, every day. Mistakes are part of your learning – mistakes are your teachers.

10 Control your emotions

Developing your mental toughness will require you to keep your thoughts and self-talk positive and avoid the habits that lead to negativity and unhealthy behaviours. The strongest people are not those who show strength in front of us but those who win battles we never see them fight. Champions are made when no one is looking!

Help yourself to prepare for whatever comes your way by maintaining your capacity to stay objective and deliver the same level of performance regardless of what you're feeling.

Find some time today to take stock of just how your uncontrolled emotions are affecting your day-to-day life. This will make it easier to identify problem areas and track your success. Your healthiest emotional state will be when you have found some balance between overwhelming emotions and no emotions at all.

11 Your compelling reason

Do you have a compelling reason to take action? Always look for the motive because it's far more powerful than the intention.

Let's say you want to lose weight to look and feel healthier. Losing weight is the intention, but looking and feeling healthier is the motive. Your motive – your compelling reason – will encourage you to resist the temptation to eat unhealthy foods in a way that the intention will not.

Today, lean on your sets of values and motives to brainstorm ideas that will help you delay immediate gratification. Your goal isn't to completely steer clear of pleasurable things – that would be a dismal way to live – but rather to develop a habit of delaying gratification.

The most effective way to develop any good habit is to take small steps. Each step you successfully take deserves a small reward and trains your brain to repeat the rewarded action.

12   Take responsibility

You are responsible. It's as easy and as complicated as that.

You're responsible for your choices, the work you put in, the work you don't put in. The wins and the losses. You're responsible for building your endurance. You are a product of your decisions, not your circumstances.

Taking ownership and responsibility for your actions is an important part of a healthy life and healthy relationships.

Taking full responsibility is a powerful reminder that you have control over the role you play in all your achievements and relationships.

Taking responsibility creates trust and dependability. You'll be able to improve your decision making, solve more problems and become more confident.

How can you take more responsibility today?

13   Embrace the unknown

By stepping out of your comfort zone you expose yourself to unfamiliar situations. It means you're moving into uncharted territory. You're trying things that you've never tried before and learning things you've never learned before.

It's only by doing this that you discover that unfamiliar situations rarely warrant fear. On the contrary, they offer opportunities to grow both personally and professionally. They give you a chance to surrender your need to control your circumstances and learn to adapt to new ones.

14   Get a sense check

It can actually be hard to recognise the things you feel most passionate about, and sometimes your purpose is more obvious to others than it is to you. It's highly likely you're already displaying your passion and purpose to the people around you without even realising it, so ask your friends and family what reminds them of you, or what they think of when you enter their mind. If you get a compliment or an observation from someone, write it down and see if any patterns emerge.

Hearing what other people notice about you might help crystallise things for you or reinforce some of the passions you've already been engaging in.

15   You're stronger than you think

It's a shame that you may never know how strong you are until being strong is the only choice you have. You are far more capable and able than you realise. You can cope with far more than you think you can. You have the ability to dig deeper and find courage and strength you never knew you had. Your capacity for coping is vast.

16   You're a winner

What separates the winners from the losers is their mental toughness, and their mindset.

A loser sees that the world is unfair, whines and complains but does nothing to improve their lot in life. A winner sees that the world is unfair but continues to struggle to improve their standing.

A winner ends up failing many times over and over but that does not stop them from getting up and persisting. What often brings you down and keeps you there is not the way you look, how rich you are or how much talent you have. What brings you down and keeps you there is your own mind.

Today, focus on the most positive aspects of every situation and adopt an optimistic, hopeful mindset.

17   You're a product of your decisions

Everyone faces drama, trauma, tragedy and obstacles in their life. It's all part of the journey, and it is rarely easy or straightforward. But it's the challenges you have faced, and are yet to face, that provide you with opportunities to grow and learn.

Even when faced with pain and sadness, you have the ability to think and behave in a positive, productive manner. The way you respond to the challenges determines the quality of your life and the achievements you make. Don't complain, don't wallow and don't feel sorry for yourself. None of these is helpful. Instead, take action because action is the only thing that can make your situation better.

Remember, you are a product of your decisions, not your circumstances.

18   Take time out

When your stress level exceeds your perceived ability to cope, take some minutes or hours of calm, reflective thought. Take a walk outdoors and breathe in the fresh air deeply. Look around you and start to notice things you've never noticed before. Your brain will welcome the extra oxygen you inhale and you'll start to think more clearly and develop a deeper sense of courage.

19   Avoid the over-optimism trap

It's good to be optimistic, and it's critical to developing mental toughness. On the flip side, if you're over-optimistic you might fail to anticipate potential obstacles and challenges, and even develop a blind spot for them.

There's no way to reliably predict everything that might go wrong, but you can guard against over-optimism by starting out with the expectation that things can, and often do, go wrong. That way, you can be prepared to respond to challenges in a productive, purposeful manner when they occur. This alone will help you to resist the impulse to give up when times get tough.

20   You can tolerate it

Successful people tend to have a much higher tolerance for pushing past discomfort and doing what needs to be done. Your ability to develop tolerance will play an important role in you achieving the success you desire.

Anything you can do to practise tolerating discomfort will help you develop focus and determination. It might be taking cold showers every day or holding a plank position for a minute. Whatever it is, when you're able to push through the initial discomfort and come out the other side, you are increasing your level of tolerance and developing your mental toughness which you can bank for the next time you have to do the hard yards.

21   You are the company you keep

They say 'you are the company you keep', so what is it that draws you to the colleagues and friends around you?

Surround yourself with positive people – choose to spend your spare time with inspirational folk who spark creativity and energy in you. Avoid people who drag you down and require you to change. It's hard to feel passionate and purposeful when you're surrounded by people who aren't making a positive contribution to your life. Talk to people in real life. Start conversations with people you don't know and be curious about what inspires and drives them. Their enthusiasm will rub off onto you.

22   Work from your point of strength

Your path to success is based on the determination you have developed and engrained within yourself. Determination is about what you're willing to do to achieve your goal. It aligns your energy and attention towards your focus.

Unhelpful distractions lead to a dimmed focus, so spend some time identifying what distracts you and stay committed to avoiding those things. This will help you become much more focused on your goal and determined to reach it. When you remove distractions, your mind has fewer choices to make it wander around, so set some boundaries and rules for yourself.

23   Who you become along the way

Setting a goal is important, but don't overlook the daily process you need to follow to get there. If you spend too much time focused on your endpoint, you risk missing the opportunities all around you.

So to achieve your goal, focus on the process of getting to it. You can't control the outcome as it involves external factors outside your control, but you can control your daily practices, actions and disciplines.

Remember, setting goals is not so much about where you end up, it's about who you become along the way.

24   Life begins outside your comfort zone

Stepping out of your comfort zone can be difficult if you don't have a compelling reason to do so, but developing mental toughness is about never settling for what you have and always looking for ways to grow.

How much do you know about the edges of your comfort zone? Are you consciously aware of what you move away from and avoid? It may not be that you avoid taking a step into the unknown and more that you don't know how far you can push yourself.

Take the time to think about what it would be like to stand on the edge of the things that create discomfort in you and take that step into uncharted territory. It will never be as bad as you anticipate. Marinate that idea long enough to build solid momentum that propels you into inspired action.

Life begins where your comfort zone ends.

25   You're right

Having self-confidence is essential to developing mental toughness. After all, it's only possible to press on during crises and adversity, to overcome the fear of uncertainty, when you trust in your abilities.

Henry Ford famously said, 'Whether you think you can or you think you can't, you're right.' He didn't dismiss the role of talent and skill but instead highlighted the role of confidence. He recognised that your self-assuredness is critical to success and that its absence can result in failure.

26   Where are the holes?

Winning is all about completing a challenge and coming out with the result you want. It's not about taking the easy way out.

Take on challenges that fit well with your beliefs and values. Wins are most likely to come when you take a slow but detailed route through the process of exploring why it's important and why it flicks your switch.

Think about what a win looks like to you. How are you going to complete this challenge? Look for the holes in your plan and think about what smart solutions you might need. Build a plan that fills those gaps.

27   Stress can be a great thing

Your mental toughness is your capacity to deal effectively with stressors, pressures, setbacks and challenges so you can perform to the best of your ability, irrespective of the circumstances in which you find yourself. Of course, it's worth remembering that not all stress is bad. In fact, stress can often help you accomplish tasks more efficiently and can even boost memory.

Stress is also a vital warning system, producing the 'fight or flight response'. When your brain perceives some kind of stress, it starts flooding the body with chemicals like epinephrine, norepinephrine and cortisol. We need good stress to stay motivated and productive. The best starting point to deal with the stress you're experiencing is to make sure you have the correct balance between good stress and bad stress. Try to take a step back from the stress you're feeling and assess the situation. React to the situation rather than to the feeling of stress. That way, you're able to handle the situation and it doesn't become stressful.

28   Find your vision

When you've identified the point to your existence here on planet Earth, your life's purpose, it will be easier for you to focus on what truly matters. You'll be better equipped to avoid the distractions that threaten to stop you achieving your vision.

Once you know your purpose, you'll see the benefits at home, at work and in social settings, but to stay focused on your goals, they have to be important to you. Your subconscious will try to trick you into believing that you want one thing, when in reality it will do very little to help you live out your purpose.

There's probably no bigger question, so spend some time thinking about this today. What vision do you have for your life?

29   What's the worst that can happen?

Even when life is good and everything is going right, self-doubt can creep in. You might begin to second-guess your decisions and hesitate before acting, in fear that you will make mistakes. Self-doubt is a natural and healthy part of your psychology. It helps you to make decisions, encourages you to do your best and protects you from negative outcomes.

The problem is, it can also paralyse you. Self-doubt can consume your thoughts, promoting fear and indecision. So, ask yourself: What is the worst that can happen if things don't go my way? The answer will reveal that mistakes are rarely disastrous. It reminds you that you can take action without fear, confident that doing so won't lead to catastrophe.

The more often you can do this, the less you'll hesitate when faced with uncertainty.

30   Do what you truly love

If you're trying to define your reason for being, look back at your past and see glimpses of things that you did as a child just for the sheer fun of it.

As you reflect on your life, you can start to pick up on certain patterns that tend to repeat themselves or some trends in the activities that you did. These patterns may hold clues to your purpose. What have you found enjoyment in for your entire life? You may have lost touch with the things that you loved as a kid. Growing up, adolescence and life generally will have dealt you a fair share of pressures that may have stripped certain passions away from you. You might believe that you should only do things that you are somehow rewarded for. The transactional nature of our society can leave you feeling disconnected from doing the things that you truly love. What is it you truly love?

CHAPTER 2

IT'S ALL ABOUT THE SELF

31   The story of the two crabs

Two crabs, a mother and a child, were walking across the sand. The mother crab scolded her child for walking wrongly and told him to walk more gracefully. The child crab explained that he didn't know how to and asked his mother to show him. The mother crab was unable to walk in the right manner herself.

The Lesson: Example is more powerful than rules and precepts. Nobody likes it when you ask them to do something that you can't even do yourself. Before making unreasonable demands, it's a good idea to be able to do it yourself first. Then you won't feel stupid for asking people do something that's impossible.

32   What's in it for me?

Think benefits instead of difficulties. Think, what's in it for me? Answering this question will help you create a positive attitude.

We're all inherently selfish and like to know how the task is likely to benefit us. More importantly, you'll see what you'll lose if you don't settle down and focus on getting the task done. It could be a failed exam, a missed deadline or a damaged reputation. Having an emotional reason for concentration will help you focus more intensely and achieve your desired outcome.

33   See yourself from the outside in

What do people ask of you when they come to you for help? Is it a specific talent that you have? Are you a great sounding board? What do people thank you for?

Appreciation from other people can help fuel your work. You may not be able to see your strengths like others do because they come naturally to you and you don't need to think about them. Look for common themes in reasons behind why people reach out to you in times of need. You might not realise the ways in which you inspire your friends to want to be like you.

34   Raise your self-esteem

Contrary to what you might think, self-esteem is entirely self-generated and you can choose to increase it, just as you can allow it to sink. Self-esteem is how you feel about yourself, the opinion you have about yourself, how you value yourself, and your perceptions about who you are and what you're capable of. With high self-esteem you'll feel more able to take risks, try new things and cope with any difficult situations that life may throw at you.

The first step in raising your self-esteem is to identify, and then challenge, a negative belief you hold about yourself. Notice your thoughts about yourself. For example, you might find yourself thinking, 'I'm not clever enough to do that' or 'I have no friends'. When you do, look for evidence that contradicts those statements. Write down both statement and evidence and keep looking back at them to remind yourself that your negative beliefs about yourself are not true.

35   Train your brain for success

Close your eyes and in your mind see the thing you're looking to achieve going exactly as you'd hope. Where are you, what are you wearing and how you do feel? Imagine how you'll respond to the various challenges you'll inevitably face, and rehearse your performance in your head.

This visualisation will literally be training your mind to expect success. Your brain does not always differentiate between real and vividly imagined experiences because the same systems in the brain are deployed for both types of experiences. When you visualise doing something successfully, your brain thinks it's real. So visualisation can literally improve your chances of success.

36   Don't put the answer in front of the question

Solving a problem should always start with asking the right questions. When you have a problem and you can't find the solution, step back and ask yourself what the real question is. Too often, we leap to looking for answers without pausing to examine the actual question.

Are you coming up with solutions without considering whether you're addressing the relevant challenges or priorities? You could be inventing fixes for things that aren't even broken.

It's all too easy to focus on what you're doing, not why you're doing it. Next time you're facing a problem, stand back and ask yourself first, what's the real question?

37   Walk right into it

Embrace what your life is trying to teach you. When you hit what you think is a breaking point, don't resist it or fight it but embrace it. Walk right into it. Often these moments are happening precisely to shine a light on what you're missing in your life and what you deeply long for.

When you learn to embrace, rather than fight, the lessons these challenging moments are trying to teach you, suddenly a new path becomes clearer and more possible than ever before.

A breakdown can indeed pave the way for a breakthrough, if you let it.

38   Do thought experiments

Ask yourself 'What if?' questions to encourage stretching your thinking style. There is never only one version of the future, so it can be really helpful to think about the multitude of possible scenarios that could develop and influence the decisions you need to make.

You'll need to be broad-minded about the possibilities that may unfold. Preparing for just one scenario risks wasting your time and energy on something that may never happen. It's better to do little thought experiments to get a wider view of the possible outcomes. This way, you may be able to determine actions that you can take today that would be valuable in many, or all, of the scenarios that might emerge tomorrow. Brainstorm with others to see what ideas they have and collect as many 'what ifs' as you can.

39   Rewrite the dictionary

Having a positive view of yourself is crucial to your performance and wellbeing. Your self-image is the mental picture you have of yourself. It's a bit like an internal dictionary that describes your characteristics – your intelligence, beauty, talent, kindness and so on. These characteristics form a collective representation of your assets (strengths) and liabilities (weaknesses) as you see them. Your childhood and life's experience will influence the image you have of yourself, and relationships will also reinforce how you feel about yourself.

Whether you see a real or a distorted image will determine whether or not you have a positive or negative self-image. Take a good look at yourself. What do you see? Are you happy with your self-image or do you need to add some words to your dictionary?

40   Manage your emotions

Mental toughness is directly connected to how you perceive yourself and your ability to perform, regardless of your circumstances. Mastering emotional control means you are able to start to recognise your emotions and understand why you're experiencing them. Once you've achieved that, you can move to learning to manage them in a healthier manner.

You don't want to disassociate yourself from your feelings because that doesn't lead to mental toughness. In the long run, disconnecting just makes you more susceptible to anxiety and depression. Managing your emotions gives you an opportunity to acknowledge them, to confront them, to scrutinise them and to decide whether what you're feeling is level-headed, given your circumstances.

Mastering your emotional control takes time, but if you can do it, it will be a major development in your mental toughness.

41   Visualise it

Successful people have fears, doubts, worries and anxieties. It's just that they don't let these feelings stand in their way. They have grit and perseverance of course, but more than that, they have the ability to visualise a future where their immediate challenges are behind them. You can use this technique, too. Imagine yourself facing challenges and overcoming them. As you start to clearly visualise the life you want, you will start to find your life reflecting your visualisations. It really works. Be open. Try it and see where it takes you!

42   Make peace with change

When you're dealing with issues in your life, you have two choices – you can accept what is happening and where you are, or you can change it. But you can't do both. However you respond, it will usually require reframing of all the thoughts, beliefs and ideas that are holding you back.

The mentally tough manage change and setbacks well. It's almost like 'water off a duck's back' for them. If you find change hard, you may experience feelings of stress and anxiety.

You might fear change, but could you learn to tolerate the pain if it meant progressing to somewhere new?

43   Watch the clock

Here are a few ideas for building your attention span:

- Sit in a chair and do nothing but sit still for 15 minutes.
- Concentrate on nothing else but slowly opening and closing your fists for five minutes.
- Follow the second hand of a clock for five minutes.

They might seem a little crazy, but you'd be surprised how hard it is to do these exercises without your mind wandering to other distractions. Practising these exercises daily will build your ability to remain focused without getting distracted.

44   Turn your thoughts into reality

Attention is the most precious resource that you can leverage to get things done. Your ability to focus on one activity will be essential if you are going to achieve your goal and get results.

Your brain is a very complex mechanism that often works without your awareness. Your subconscious mind, the deep place where all your memories, feelings and neuro-associations are stored, can be your best friend or your worst enemy. Your thoughts shape your reality because your thoughts generate feelings, feelings lead to action and action leads to results.

Set yourself one critical task to achieve today, visualise yourself completing the task and simulate the feelings you'll get after finishing the task. If you truly think about your day's success, your subconscious will do everything it can to help turn your thoughts into reality.

45   Watch out for the F word

You might fear failure. You might fear success. You might fear the unfamiliar and the unknown, regardless of its form.

Fear can sabotage your resilience, it can erode your resolve, and it can release unhealthy emotions that cause you to focus on potentially negative outcomes. Fear takes every potentially negative outcome and amplifies its impact. You can freeze up, overwhelmed by the possibility of disaster. Fear distorts reality. It implies that catastrophe and ruination are certain to follow your performance.

If you allow fear to gain a foothold in your mind, you'll end up feeling defeated before you've even started to take any action. The truth is, the odds of catastrophe resulting from whatever you're doing are so tiny that they're unworthy of consideration.

46   The power of conscientiousness

Conscientious people achieve more because they are thorough, careful and vigilant. If you're conscientiousness, you will have a desire to complete a task well, be efficient and organised, and not want to rest until the job is done and done right. You'll also have strong moral principles and values – you'll want to do the right thing. Conscientious people are dedicated to work and are capable of intense, single-minded effort. Conscientious people stick to their convictions and opinions and opposition only serves to strengthen their dogged determination. How can you improve your conscientiousness?

47   Safeguard your self-image

It's possible that your single most important characteristic is how you feel about yourself.

Your self-image is considered to be made up of 85 per cent your attitude and 15 per cent your skills. People who genuinely like and accept themselves as valuable individuals perform at a higher level of effectiveness than others.

Your self-image is how you think about yourself and is based on your thoughts and information you have stored in your subconscious. These thoughts have created and formed certain feelings about yourself that lead you to behave in certain ways. Allow yourself lots of positive input, as your positive experiences will increase your personal sense of confidence.

48   Learn from Jay Shetty

Award winning storyteller and podcaster, Jay Shetty, was born into a family whose expectation was that he would become a lawyer, a doctor, or a failure.

Jay refused to be pressured by his parents and chose to follow his purpose in life – to do something meaningful that would impact the world. He turned down two amazing corporate job offers when he graduated from business school. Instead, he lived and trained as a monk, committing 'career suicide'. He shaved his hair, wore robes and lived out of a gym locker for three years. He describes his time as a monk as one of the best experiences of his life.

Don't accept the pressure to travel in a certain direction through life. Think less about *what* you want to be, and more about *who* you want to be.

49   Use your windscreen

When you're driving, you use the rearview mirror as a reference point for what's happening behind you. You use the windscreen to see ahead and move forward because you can scan the distance and make plans for every action you take. Remember this driving analogy when it comes to your life.

If you spend your life staring into the past (the rearview mirror) for long periods, you will eventually crash. Embrace your past as just that – your past. It is gone, and it is behind you. You can register your past as simply a reference point; it should not determine your present or your future.

Your windscreen is much bigger than your rearview mirror for a very good reason.

50   Use the negatives positively

Use your negative emotions to propel you forward. Negative emotions are completely normal and healthy and they have important benefits, too. Negative emotions like sadness and grief help you to communicate with others who need support and kindness. Negative emotions like anger can help motivate you to take action, make changes in your life, or maybe even change the world.

At their root, emotions are designed to direct your behaviour in important ways. Casually pushing negative emotions aside without reflecting on where they come from can leave you stuck and unable to move forward in the ways you desire. So when life throws you into a ditch and you feel down, ask yourself, 'Is this negative emotion trying to teach me something?' Would pushing the negative emotion away leave whatever is causing this negative emotion intact? Must something be done to stop this negative emotion from emerging again in the future? So don't push the emotion away – use it to fuel change in your life, or in the world.

Pay attention to see if your negative emotions are trying to lead you in a positive direction. Then decide for yourself whether to follow or not.

51 Keep on keeping on

Winston Churchill famously urged people to keep going, even if they were facing hellish obstacles. You probably associate perseverance with pain and suffering, but when you have true grit, you'll be able to flip your perspective on perseverance 180 degrees and view struggle as a doorway to pleasure. When you know how to persevere you can start and continue on the path towards any goal you set, and that may well be the difference between failure and success.

But the difference between someone who succeeds and someone who just spends a lot of time doing something is that your practice must have purpose. Set long-term goals that can provide the context and framework in which to find the meaning and value of your long-term efforts. From struggles comes strength, and your endeavour will cultivate the drive, sustainability, passion, courage, stamina… and true grit to get you there.

52 Trigger happy habit-forming

In order to develop good habits, you must have a clear idea about how to trigger them and what kinds of things are likely to trigger you to break them.

A trigger is an event that kicks off the automatic urge to complete a habit. Triggers are the key to forming new habits and breaking old ones. Simply put, triggers make the habit action happen. At the core of every habit is a loop that consists of three parts: a cue, a routine and a reward. A cue might be a location, a time of day, other people, or an emotional state. A routine is the behaviour you wish to change (e.g. smoking or biting your nails). A reward is the reason your brain decides the previous steps are worth remembering for the future – it provides positive reinforcement for the desired behaviour, making it more likely that you will produce that behaviour again in the future.

So identify a new habit you wish to adopt and write down the cue, route and reward to prevent being triggered back to bad habits.

53 Learn to listen

Your right ear is connected to the left side of the brain, which is the language and logical centre. This means that your hearing is superior in the right ear, so try to use this for listening. When you are listening to someone, give them your total and undivided attention. Don't let your eyes, or indeed your mind, wander elsewhere while the other person is talking. Apart from anything else this demonstrates courtesy, interest and respect. Focus on what the person is saying and give no attention to anything else. Don't interrupt, and don't finish the other person's sentence. Keep the conversation going by asking intelligent, relevant questions that show you are tuned in and paying attention to them. It is much easier to talk than to listen. Deep listening will improve your concentration skills and in the process you may make friends and learn something new.

54 Track it back

It's believed that you will have over 50,000 thoughts a day. That's a lot of input, especially when you think about how the quality and content of those 50,000 thoughts will impact how you see yourself. Those thoughts will also impact how you feel about yourself and how you choose to behave.

The self-talk in your head creates feelings in you, which then lead to your behaviour. It's impossible to have feelings without thoughts, so if you ever wondered why you behaved in a certain way, you can easily go back and check out what you were feeling. After establishing your feelings, identify your thoughts and from there you can start to understand the reason for your behaviour.

55 Tolerate your emotions

To build your self-confidence you'll need to acquire an awareness of your emotions. This also requires that you build a tolerance to them.

The only way to do so is to expose yourself to the discomfort that accompanies negative emotions. Many of us tend to suppress emotional pain, but you should remain open to this experience as doing so helps you to build resilience. Building resilience allows you to remain attuned to negative emotions without being paralysed by them.

56 Step into uncharted territory

If you want something you've never had, you must do something you've never done. You're going to have to break new ground, step into uncharted territory and try things you've never attempted before. You're going to have to put your neck on the line, take risks and be bold. See this as exciting rather than daunting and scary.

57 Today is special

Burn the candles, use the nice sheets, wear your smart clothes. Don't save anything for a special occasion. Celebrate every birthday because some people don't get to reach that age. Life is full of surprises. You'll never know for certain what your future will hold or how it will look. You'll never know where you'll end up or what you'll accomplish in the next few years. You'll never know who you will befriend, what you will experience, how you will feel.

Life is full of happiness – strangers helping each other through tough times, friends sharing fun and memorable moments, people working together to make life better. But of course, life is also full of sadness and setbacks. The people you love will suffer and die. You could lose all your money, or have your reputation damaged. Life is a fluctuating experience. It won't always go your way. You cannot have good without having seen the bad.

Today is a gift, that's why it's called the present.

58   Training for the future

Have you allowed your past to define you? Have you allowed earlier events, along with your responses to them, to decide who you are today? Your values and convictions are often intertwined with what has happened before in your life.

Learn to sever this connection and condition your mind to view your past as nothing more than 'training for the future'. Things happened and you responded. You may have made mistakes but now it's time to use your past as a learning tool – an instruction manual – that provides you with insight into how best to respond down the road.

59   Welcome failure

When someone decides they want to avoid failure, what they are really saying is they want to avoid success. Failure brings the opportunity to learn things better. It helps you to learn from your mistakes. Failures must be embraced because they make you rethink and reconsider, so you can find new ways and strategies to achieve your goals. Failure helps you gain a deeper experience and better knowledge that will serve you well.

Just like success and failure, there is light and darkness, the sun and the moon, life and death. They are inseparable and to have one is to accept the other. Today, accept the relationship between success and failure. You'll quickly realise there is no need to fear failure. Failure is not a sign that something was not meant for you, nor is it a sign that you are inadequate in some way. Failure is a sign that you are on a journey to change your life.

60   Time to reboot

Would you regret giving up? Ask yourself this question regularly. How will you feel in the future about the decisions you make today? Will future you have no regrets, or will you kick yourself for making a poor decision?

If you think you'll regret it, this is the time to review your commitment rather than surrender to the impulse to give up. There's nothing wrong with abandoning a task if it's no longer in line with your longer-term goal. But if you're tempted to give up due to lack of resilience, ask yourself what you can do to reboot your commitment.

CHAPTER 3

TOUGH TALK

61   The story of the tired bird

A tired bird landed on a branch. The bird rested, enjoying the view from the branch and the protection it offered from dangerous animals. Just as the bird became used to the branch and the support and safety it offered, a strong wind started blowing and the tree swayed with such intensity that it seemed the branch would snap in half. But the bird was not worried for it knew two important truths. The first truth: even without the branch it was able to fly and thus remain safe through the power of its own two wings. The second truth: it also knew that there were many other branches on which it could temporarily rest.

The Lesson: This story tells you a lot about your self-confidence and courage. You are capable of so much more than you realise, and when you can release your grasp on the physical structures that hold you to the ground, then you start to understand just how far you can fly under your own power.

62   Find your flow

You may have heard people say, 'Time flies when you're having fun.' Moments like this are what psychologists call the 'flow' and what spiritual people call connecting with the divine. Whatever is the case for you, when time is flying, you've found where your passions are. You are fulfilling your purpose when you are doing something that energises you rather than something that drains your energy and leaves you feeling exhausted. When you are living your purpose, you are not left wondering, 'Is it 5 p.m. yet?'

63   Thought stopping

You can use 'thought stopping' to eliminate negative self-talk. Thought stopping is recognising that you are thinking something unhelpful and you want to change it.

As soon as you recognise a negative thought, you need to literally say to yourself 'stop' and replace the negative with a positive thought. Some people like to put a rubber band on their wrist and pop it every time they notice a negative thought.

Controlling your negative self-talk gets easier as you learn to recognise when it's occurring, and just like anything else, the more you do it, the easier it becomes.

And you need to get good at it because they say it takes 11 positive thoughts to cancel one negative one.

64   Unlimit yourself

Moving out of your comfort zone forces you to develop new skills. One of the many benefits you'll experience is that you'll be stepping away from your 'limited set of behaviours' and you'll start to develop your ability and expertise in new areas.

Living inside your comfort zone requires only a limited skill set and those skills won't contribute much to your success. Once you can confidently step outside of your comfort zone and learn a host of new skills, there'll be no limit to how much you can achieve.

65   There's a patch for that

What if you could tell you when you needed to drink more water or reach for a sports drink?

Sweat is easy to stimulate and has a rich chemical composition, making it an ideal body fluid to measure health and athletic performance. There are sticky patches you can use which collect sweat at the surface of the skin and analyse it, giving you the signal to rehydrate.

Knowing your sweat rate and sweat composition could help you to decide how much you need to drink to rehydrate and replenish your body, keeping you in tip-top physical and mental condition throughout the day.

66   The virtue that is patience

Patience could be described as your capacity to accept or tolerate delay, problems or suffering without becoming annoyed or anxious. We all lose our patience occasionally, but doing so frequently or inappropriately can harm your reputation, damage your relationships, increase stress or escalate a difficult situation. Patience is a virtue!

Whatever the obstacle you have to overcome, it will likely require determination and focus to achieve. And you'll need to manage your emotions throughout the journey. These emotions can range from eagerness to get it done to anger at the frustrations you encounter along the way, which could cause you to become demotivated. So, don't expect results immediately or rush things to fruition before their time. Anything worthwhile takes hard work and endurance – view everything as a work in progress.

67   The value of values

You must know that to become mentally tough you need to be acutely aware of what you feel deep down, your thoughts, beliefs and convictions. You must clarify your values so that your responses to unfavourable circumstances are purposeful.

Your values are your beliefs about what's important or what matters most to you in life. They determine your priorities and, deep down, they're probably the measures you use to tell whether your life is turning out the way you want it to. When the things that you do and the way you behave match your values, life is usually good – you're satisfied and content. But when they don't align with your personal values, that's when things feel wrong. This can be a real source of unhappiness, so make a conscious effort to identify your values.

What values are important to you?

68 The sky's the limit

With everything that happens once you move out of your comfort zone, you're naturally going to achieve more than ever before. Your increased concentration and focus will help you develop new skills. Those new skills will change the way you see yourself, encouraging you to step even further out of your comfort zone.

69 Be clear about the payoff

Everything you do, you do with purpose. You work towards achieving a particular outcome because that outcome carries a reward that is important to you. You eat healthy food because it's good for your body. You lose weight to have more energy. You invest your time, effort and emotions into particular relationships because you want those relationships to be rewarding.

When you're clear about the rewards you'll enjoy for your efforts, you're more inclined to enjoy the hardships you face along the way. When these rewards are unclear, you're more inclined to give up. You might ask yourself, 'What is the point of enduring this misery?'

Be clear about the payoff, the end goal, because this will help you to resist the urge to give up when you face setbacks.

70   The only way out is through

You only do what you tolerate, but tolerance is the key to your success. Successful people have a much higher tolerance for always being 'on', for pushing past discomfort and doing what needs to be done. The ones that get ahead tolerate an immense amount of discomfort, so much so that it no longer becomes uncomfortable. The only way out is through.

You can build your tolerance level by doing an exaggerated amount of a thing for as long as you can. So, pick one thing to do today and do that thing every day for two weeks. See how you quickly you adjust and start to tolerate discomfort more easily every day.

You could try holding the plank position, holding your hand in ice-cold water, smiling when you don't feel like smiling, speaking up when you normally wouldn't, or eating food you would normally avoid.

71   The power of choice

You may not be able to control what happens to you but you can control how you respond to it.

Resilient people are not afraid to acknowledge their negative feelings, emotions and fears. Instead, they choose not to let these negative fears and emotions take control and immobilise them.

Resilient people know that they are not responsible for the challenging events in their lives. They also know they are in control of their responses to these events.

Resilient people are comfortable with using the power of choice. They understand its value when dealing with tough decisions or confronting challenging situations.

By embracing the power of choice, you will be able to maintain perspective and manage the flow of emotions that you're dealing with in the present moment. Using the power of choice empowers and strengthens your ability to take action and to make decisions.

72   The one you feed will win

An old Cherokee was teaching his grandchildren about life. He said, 'A battle is raging inside me... it is a terrible fight between two wolves. One wolf represents fear, anger, envy, sorrow, regret, greed, arrogance, self-pity, guilt, resentment, inferiority, lies, false pride, superiority and ego. The other stands for joy, peace, love, hope, sharing, serenity, humility, kindness, benevolence, friendship, empathy, generosity, truth, compassion and faith.'

The old man looked at the children with a firm stare. 'This same fight is going on inside you, and inside every other person, too.'

They thought about it for a minute, then one child asked his grandfather, 'Which wolf will win?' The old Cherokee replied: 'The one you feed.'

73   The importance of trust

Trust is a critical element in all relationships, personal or professional. Without trust you don't have a 'team', you have a group of individuals, working together, often making disappointing progress. When trust is in place, each individual in a group becomes stronger because they feel part of an effective, cohesive group.

When people truly trust one another, they can achieve truly meaningful goals. Trust is essential to any relationship because it provides a sense of safety and security. When people feel safe with each other, they feel comfortable to open up, take appropriate risks and expose vulnerabilities.

How can you build trust in your relationships today?

74   Passion beats intelligence

Success doesn't come easy. It's not supposed to be easy. It's supposed to be hard. For everyone. We'd all be billionaires or Olympic athletes if success came easy. Hard work, resilience, grit and drive are the timeless qualities that will propel you to where you want to be. Your mental toughness will be your game changer.

All the things you can't see, hold, photograph or buy are the things that will set you apart from the rest. It is not your skill or intelligence that will be your biggest ally. Your determination, passion, focus, confidence and bounce-back ability will get you to where you want to be. Start developing these things today and you're going to be in great shape to succeed.

75   It's all about what you can't see

Your mental toughness will play a bigger part than anything else in you achieving success. It is not your training or how clever you are that will make the difference to your success, it is your mental toughness – your ability to keep going without giving up, despite whatever is going on around you, that will be the game changer for you.

76   Adapt and flex

Darwin said, 'It is not the most intellectual of the species that survives, it is not the strongest that survives, but the species that survives is the one that is able best to adapt and adjust to the changing environment in which it finds itself.' The same goes for you.

Disruption isn't new, but the speed, the complexity and the modern nature of disruption are on a scale we've never seen before. Life is a game where the rules and goals are constantly changing – the long-term winners aren't those who simply try to make it to the next level but the ones who continually adapt.

To be successful you will need to continually adapt to take advantage of your changing environment. Being strong is important, useful and helpful, but you need to develop the ability to adapt and flex to the challenges and setbacks you face every day.

77   The clue is in your body

There's a time and place for everything, including intense emotions. Sobbing uncontrollably is a pretty common response to losing a loved one. Screaming into your pillow (or punching it) might help you relieve some anger and tension after being dumped. Other situations, however, will call for some restraint or management.

No matter how frustrated you are, screaming at your boss over an unfair disciplinary action won't help. Being mindful of your surroundings and the situation can help you learn when it's OK to let feelings out and when you might want to sit with them for the moment.

Sitting with your feelings means simply that you pay attention to your body's sensations that occur alongside the emotion. When you feel happy, you may feel an openness in your chest, but if you feel anxious, you might feel knots in your stomach. Sit with your emotions for 10 minutes to understand how your body is reacting to the emotion you're feeling.

78   The Chinese bamboo tree

Like any plant, the Chinese bamboo tree requires nurturing – water, fertile soil, sunshine. In its first year you'll see no visible growth or signs of activity. In the second year, again, you'll see no growth above the soil and you'll wonder why you're bothering. You invest time and effort for no reward. And finally, in the fifth year, something amazing happens: the Chinese bamboo tree grows 8 feet in just six weeks!

Don't give up on your dreams – keep going, relentlessly; it will all pay back.

79   The easiest path

When you encounter obstacles, your mind immediately looks for the path of least resistance – the easiest path.

That's rational – why should you put in more effort than necessary to achieve the desired outcome? Why should you endure more stress than necessary? Why should you put yourself through distress and discomfort if there's no need to?

The problem is, there are countless distractions offering simpler paths and you can even be distracted by easier goals. You may find yourself looking for activities that pose less trouble and come with fewer complications.

Fortunately, you can train yourself to ignore distractions; it just takes time, just as developing any good habit does. Check that your goal is not too big that you'll get discouraged, or so easy that it doesn't challenge you.

80   Emotion versus logic

Willpower is your ability to resist short-term temptations to meet your long-term goals. You can see it as a battle between your logic and your emotions. It's your self-control saying 'no' to too much eating, spending, phone scrolling, drinking alcohol and other indulgences that keep you from staying on track to reach your goals.

Willpower is something we all wish we had more of. One of the ways you can restore your willpower is to manage your stress levels. As willpower is emotional in nature, when you're stressed, negative emotions are released and your willpower gets diminished. As a result, you're unable to perform effectively when you need to.

Don't forget your willpower may get fatigued in the short term but it can be strengthened over time, just like your muscles when you exercise. So to increase this valuable source of strength, you need to manage your stress in such a way that it reduces. Today, use breathing exercises or meditation when you feel your will power diminishing.

81   Tell the truth

Tell everyone about your goals. Many people will argue that you should keep your goals private, but I am not sure that's true. It takes courage to be open about your goals. It takes courage to be open about your failings. Radical openness and honesty will be crucial to your success and to moving forward in your life.

All progress starts by telling the truth. Honesty is not just about telling the truth; it's also about being real with yourself and others about who you are, what you want and what you need to live an authentic life. Honesty sharpens your perception and allows you to observe everything around you with clarity.

82   This is a hijack

Negative emotions are not in themselves unhealthy. Research shows that negative emotions contribute to mental health and psychological wellbeing, so it pays to acknowledge them.

Having said that, negative emotions can easily hijack your ability to make rational decisions and take purposeful action. They can quickly overwhelm you. So it pays to assess whether the anger, shame, sadness, panic or guilt you experience is overblown.

You don't want to suppress negative emotions, but it's important to develop the habit of investigating them the moment they surface.

83   Tap it away

Tapping, also known as EFT (Emotional Freedom Technique), is used to heal emotional pain. You use your fingertips to stimulate energy points on the body, and while this does sound a bit out there, it's been scientifically proven that the tapping technique rewires the brain by sending calming signals to the amygdala, the stress centre of the brain. This allows both the body and the brain to release self-imposed limitations from negative experiences, emotions, thoughts and the stuff that holds you back from creating the life you want.

Choose a simple phrase to repeat while you tap, using your fingertips, five times in these areas: the top of your head; the outer side of your eyes; at the the start of your eyebrows, just above the nose; under your eyes; the depression under your nose and above the upper lip (the philtrum); and on your chin.

84   Mind your language

Visualisation is your ability to see pictures in your head, and self-talk is the dialogue you have going on in your head. If you learn any skill from this book, the most important is understanding the relationship between how you think and how you feel and behave.

The difference between your best and worst performance lies within your mind and thoughts. Yes, really. It's vital you're aware of your continuous internal dialogue, when you're literally telling yourself what to think and feel about whatever is happening around you.

You don't have total control over what you think, but you can choose to change what you say to yourself. This is one of your most important choices.

85   Take daily action

Rome wasn't built in a day, and the life you want to create won't happen in one day either. But adopting a series of daily actions that move you towards your goal will bring your dreams to reality.

Don't get too caught up with how far you have to go; instead, focus on the present and set yourself daily or weekly actions to get to where you want to be. Taking regular actions that move you towards your goal will work. Trust in the process.

86   Take an ice-cold shower

In order to build resilience and determination you will need to start practising tolerating discomfort.

We all default to the easy and comfortable, but that teaches us nothing new and moves us no further forward. When you are prepared to experience discomfort, you will start to discover how much you can cope with. So try this… Take an ice-cold shower for three minutes every day for seven days. You can do anything for three minutes! The freezing-cold water will trigger a stress response and you will start to hyperventilate.

Your heart rate will shoot up and you'll be flooded with adrenaline. Over time (even a few days) your body will adapt and your stress response will fall. The cold water activates the body's natural healing powers, makes you more alert, boosts your mood, aids digestion, weight loss, improved sleep, and strengthens your immune system. Many people do this every day of the year as they feel so many benefits.

When you know you can tolerate the discomfort of a three-minute ice-cold shower, you will be building resilience and mental toughness.

87   Talk to yourself

Self-affirmations like 'I can do this' and 'I've got what it takes' help to increase your self-confidence and belief in your own abilities. They work because simple statements help to shift your focus away from perceived failures and direct your focus towards your strengths. Creating a mental image of yourself doing something activates many of the same brain areas that *actually* experiencing these situations would.

Using affirmations can help you feel more relaxed before an event because you've mentally rehearsed and feel fully prepared, so you're less likely to have self-sabotaging thoughts or behaviours that could potentially interfere with your success.

Repeating an affirmation will help to boost your motivation and confidence, but you still have to take some action yourself. Try thinking of affirmations as a step towards change, not as the change itself.

88   Take a mental break

Taking a mental break from work and spending some time looking after yourself can sometimes give you the mini-break you need so that you can return with a clear head. Changing the scene or changing the pace is good for your mental health, so you might pick up your favourite book, sing to the music on the radio, or sit quietly and meditate for a few minutes.

A mini-break doesn't necessarily mean you'll be able to fix that problem, but it can protect you from feeling overwhelmed by it.

Resilient people bounce back and fight back where they can, but they also learn to take a mental break. What's your favourite way to take a mental break?

89   Develop your laser focus

Your laser focus will shift you from ordinary to extraordinary. If you want to succeed, you have to find strategies to help you focus, despite all of the distractions that threaten to prevent you from doing the task at hand.

Thankfully, developing laser-like focus is easier than you'd think. First, make sure you're sleeping well and getting regular exercise. These are the basis of productivity, performance and focus.

Next, check the temperature of the room because research shows that people who work in a room set to around 70 degrees Fahrenheit (21 °C) are more successful and focused than people in colder work spaces.

Do not be tempted to multitask or constantly switch between tasks, as this actually has a negative effect on your ability to focus.

Ironically, taking breaks can help improve your focus as they restore motivation.

90   Take a giant leap

To develop your mental toughness, you must know, deep down, what you're feeling. You need to be acutely aware of your feelings, thoughts, beliefs and convictions. You need to clarify your values so that your responses to unfavourable circumstances are purposeful.

To build mental toughness, you don't need to detach yourself from your feelings but instead embrace them. By acknowledging your fear and frustration when things go wrong, you'll be able to evaluate their veracity or accuracy, and regulate what's not realistic.

When you increase your self-awareness, you will be taking a giant leap towards emotional mastery.

CHAPTER 4

BODY BOOSTING

91   The story of the stag and the hunter

A stag was drinking at a river, admiring its beautiful antlers in its reflection. He noticed how small and weak his legs looked. Just then, out of nowhere, a hunter approached and shot an arrow. The stag ran away into the woods and realised that it was thanks to his legs that he had survived.

The Lesson: We often despise what is most useful to us. Our greatest weaknesses can also be our greatest strengths – a way of us fitting into the world.

92   Sweat it out

Your body has about 3 million sweat glands. The density of sweat glands varies across your body, the highest being on your forehead and cheeks, your palms and fingers as well as on the soles of your feet. So, your skin – and how much it sweats – can tell you a lot about how you are feeling when you're exposed to emotionally loaded events or other stimuli, both positive and negative.

No matter whether you're stressed, nervous, fearful, psyched up, excited, baffled or surprised, whenever you're emotionally aroused, sweat glands are triggered and become more active. They secrete moisture through pores towards the skin's surface and you can measure the electrical conductivity of the sweat with a 'galvanic skin response' sensor. So now you can actually measure how well you are managing the stress and pressure you're facing.

93   Start dreaming big

Set yourself a goal that will enable you to explore your abilities and stretch yourself. Dreaming big means you'll have the mental freedom to think about what you really want out of life and forget about all the reasons why you can't make it a reality. Dreaming big will motivate you to see the bigger picture. You'll find out that you're able to handle all kinds of challenges.

Your dreams encompass your goals, but they also give your life purpose, direction and meaning. They shape your choices, help you build towards the future and give you a sense of control and hope.

94   Feed your brain

Your brain needs proper food to thrive and survive. Despite its small size in relation to your total body weight, it needs a disproportionate amount of energy and nutrients to keep functioning healthily. It uses more energy than any other body organ, accounting for up to 20 per cent of the body's total.

What you eat and drink significantly affects the way your brain works and how it retains its focus and concentration. Your brain needs plenty of water to keep dehydrated – even mild dehydration results in shrinkage of brain tissue and temporary loss of concentration and memory. A little caffeine can improve concentration, alertness and productivity. But remember, caffeine is a psychoactive drug, so don't overdo it!

95   Stop comparing

It happens all the time: you're happy with your job until you hear about someone else's and it sounds much better. You're happy with the growth of your business until you hear of someone else's growing faster. You feel like things are going pretty well until a peer does something you'd love to do.

If you compare your life to anything other than a former version of itself, you're asking for unhappiness. Even some of the most successful and inspiring people have moments when they want to swap places with someone else. It's madness. Of course there are other things you could be doing, but choosing to do them would mean forgoing your current path.

Keep to your path or you'll end up flitting around with no agenda, copying the last success story you read on the internet. Make comparisons with no one but your former self.

96   Support yourself

Taking good care of yourself is key to maintaining motivation and achieving your goals. A lack of energy might relate to a failure to look after your inner support system, which provides the physical, emotional and mental energy you'll need to achieve the goals you've set.

Make sure you are eating healthily and review your diet with a fresh set of eyes. You're only as healthy as the food and drink you put into your body, so be sure to eat plenty of fibre, vegetables and fruit. Your body is 60 per cent water and will dehydrate really quickly if you don't drink enough water every day – set a target of drinking 2 litres of water each day.

97   Stress testing

A large part of developing your mental toughness will involve cognitive restructuring. This is the process of questioning all the negative, inaccurate thoughts, attitudes and emotions you harbour. It's about changing how you view the world as well as your place in it rather than accepting your automatic reactions to your circumstances and trusting them as reasonable or rational. You can put your thoughts under the microscope and scrutinise them.

Cognitive restructuring isn't a once-and-done process, at least not in the context of developing your mental toughness. It's something you'll need to attend on a daily basis, monitoring your thoughts and stress-testing them for validity.

98 Stop saying yes

One sure-fire formula for disaster is trying to please everyone. It's easy to become a people pleaser because you want everyone to like you and you dread disapproval. Pleasing everyone seems to be a safe way to avoid conflict and confrontation, but remind yourself that if you don't speak up and say what's on your mind, you are not being the real you.

By always trying to please, you run the risk of changing your plans to suit others, extending your workload and getting trapped in a spiralling cycle of always saying yes. It may be well intentioned, but you will be hiding what you really think, and that's not truthful! You need to be strong to achieve your goals, and strong people seek strong people to be around.

99 The power of optimistic thinking

I worry about encouraging 'positive thinking' because there's always a danger of pretending something is good when it isn't. Being over-positive could force you to cover up or silence a bad experience. Pain, worry, heartbreak and fear are all normal emotions and unavoidable aspects of being a human.

Instead, try to build some *optimistic* thinking into your life. Optimistic thinking is about feeling hopeful and positive about the future, believing things will get better. Optimists expect good things to happen, whereas pessimists expect or predict unfavourable outcomes.

Are you an optimist or a pessimist? What can you start to feel more hopeful about today?

100   Stop a moment

They say patience is a virtue and it's true. Patience can help you achieve your goals, maintain a more positive outlook on life and make you less reactive, which in turn will make you less prone to bad decisions. Stress, regret and anger don't help anyone or anything.

So when you're facing an uncertain future, a negative event or something scary, take a minute. Don't do anything. Just sit for a moment. And if you find your brain veering in a negative direction, remind yourself of the positive things about life to get yourself back in the right frame of mind to make better decisions. Remember, as they say, good things come to those who wait.

101   Own your mistakes

Mentally tough people own their mistakes. They never try to pretend they didn't happen. Pretending it didn't happen is the typical stance people take when they know they've done something wrong. Instead of just owning the error, they attempt (unsuccessfully) to defend their position, which only digs the hole deeper and leads to loss of trust and deterioration of relationships.

Instead of being too proud to say you're wrong, accept full responsibility for your actions. Admitting your mistakes frees you from guilt. By not admitting you're wrong, you allow the guilt to sit and rot in your stomach.

102   The big sleep

Are you sleeping enough? Just like eating, sleep is necessary for your survival. Sleep gives your body a rest and allows it to prepare for the next day. It's like giving your body a mini-holiday. Scientists think that sleep is probably the time when your brain sorts and stores information, replaces chemicals and solves problems. If you're not getting enough sleep, you might experience poor memory and focus, weakened immunity and mood changes. Most adults need around seven to nine hours of sleep each night. 'Early to bed and early to rise makes a man healthy, wealthy, and wise.' Are you getting your quota?

Caffeine can significantly worsen sleep quality, especially if you drink large amounts in the late afternoon or evening. Stay away from caffeine, alcohol and nicotine to immediately improve the quality and quantity of your sleep.

103   Stay with hungry

Developing mental toughness will require you to practise controlling your impulses. It makes you yearn for something more, teaches you to adapt and grow. It forces you to change, stretch and find new strategies. So, your challenge today to help you develop this strength is when you feel hungry, wait an extra 15 minutes before you eat. It's OK to be hungry, and you know you're going to eat. So rather than rushing in and eating on impulse, sit with the hunger feeling. The more often you can do this, the easier it will become to tolerate discomfort.

104   Take courage

When you think of courage, you probably think of physical bravery, but it comes in many other forms. After all, courage is not the absence of fear but the triumph over it. Courage is taking a chance when others would not, following your vision no matter where it takes you, standing up for what you believe in, especially when your beliefs are unpopular, or simply doing the right thing even though easier options exist.

So today, have the courage to be patient, to believe the unbelievable, to forgive and move on quickly, to stay the course when everyone else has abandoned ship, to say no, or to ask for help.

105   Enjoy your successes

Naturally, once you commit 100 per cent to your goal, you'll start enjoying small successes along the way. Each success you have will fuel your confidence and make you even more formidable. Start to rack up these successes and enjoy the feeling of every little one, however small.

Procrastinating or getting sidetracked with distractions has nothing on the feeling of banking these small victories, which compound over time to make you even more determined, more focused and more confident in your abilities. You know you can do this, so stay committed, focused and determined.

106   Start talking

There's a big difference between 'being strong' and 'acting tough'. Acting tough is about pretending you don't have any problems. Being strong is about admitting you don't have all the answers.

While it might feel uncomfortable, talking to someone can help you develop mental toughness and become better. So, make a concerted effort to reach out and talk to your friends and family regularly. A close friend or family member can give you a different perspective on what you're experiencing.

Be open to seeking professional help, too. Start with talking to your doctor to rule out physical health problems and then get a referral to a mental health professional. These days you can text, video chat or talk on the phone with a therapist.

107   The story of the north wind and the sun

The wind and the sun were arguing over who was stronger. Suddenly, they saw a traveller coming along the road. They decide to settle the argument with a challenge: whoever could get the traveller to take off his coat would be the winner. The wind blew as hard as it could, but the traveller just tightened his coat even more. Then the sun softly shone its rays on him. The traveller began to feel hot until finally he removed his coat.

The Lesson: Persuasion is better than force. A kind, gentle manner like the sun showed is always better than cold threats and force. So, if you ever need something from someone, be kind and humble rather than yelling at them. As you will find, they always respond better.

108   Start a chain reaction

Kindness is one of the only things that doubles when you share it! Science has shown that if you perform just one random act of kindness a day, it will reduce your stress levels, anxiety or sadness. Your body will be flooded with hormones that will make you, and the person you've helped, feel calmer and happier. Serotonin makes you feel good, endorphins reduce pain, and oxytocin reduces your blood pressure and makes you feel more loving and loved.

So an act of kindness will boost your feelings of confidence, being in control, happiness and optimism. It'll also encourage others to repeat the good deeds they've experienced themselves and make them feel amazing, too. Start a chain reaction!

109   Stand tall

First impressions are everything. People will make a judgement about you in a fraction of a second, and if you're not careful, you can project a very different image than what you intend. Projecting an air of confidence means you're much more likely to build trust and rapport quickly. You can't see or touch confidence, but you can definitely feel it and sense it.

So today, stand, and sit, two inches taller than you normally would. One inch is easy – two inches is more of a stretch. This assertive posture means you'll immediately feel your chest rise, which will open your airways and allow oxygen to flow more easily, and you will be displaying a whole new air of confidence about yourself.

110   Stress can be your ally

Your stress response is your body's effort to cope with external risks and threats. It's your body's vital warning sign, protecting you from danger by increasing your heart rate to prepare you to act. So rather than worry that your stress response might screw everything up, start to see it as an ally. Stress can work for you, sharpening your reactions, focusing your mind and preparing you for action. When you can reframe the stress you're experiencing not as an outside enemy but as an opportunity to rise to the occasion, then you will be building your mental toughness.

Embrace the feelings of stress and use them to accomplish more and stay motivated.

111   Sssh that voice

You have an inner critic – we all do. It's the voice in your head telling you that you're not good enough, or smart enough, or attractive enough. It's the voice that tries to convince you that you don't deserve the success you seek. It finds fault in everything you do and demands that others do the same.

Your inner critic may prove to be your most challenging adversary as you develop mental toughness. That internal voice will not only dwell on the negative aspects of your performance – both perceived and real – it'll try to get you to do the same. Once your mind is focused on negativity, your inner critic will have successfully distracted you from strengthening your resolve.

Becoming mentally tough requires you to silence your negative self-talk.

112   Spring back into shape

The term 'resilience' is actually borrowed from engineering, where it refers to the ability of a substance or object to spring back into shape. In the same way that a material object would require strength and flexibility in order to bounce back, you, too, require these characteristics to be resilient. When you are resilient you will adapt well in the face of adversity, trauma, tragedy, threats or even significant sources of stress.

Accept that difficulties, challenges and change are all part of life and living. Focus on the things that you can change or influence instead of the things that are out of your control.

113   Find the good in the bad

Sometimes tragedy and trauma can result in great learnings and personal growth. It may be hard to see it at the time, but living through a difficult situation can increase your self-confidence and sense of self-worth, strengthen your relationships and teach you a great deal about yourself.

Many people who have experienced hardship have reported a heightened appreciation for life and deepened gratitude. In many situations there will be a 'silver lining' (when something good comes out of something bad) or nugget of gold hidden in there that will give meaning to the event and help you to move forward. These findings and realisations are what you'll need to create energy to pick yourself up and go again.

114   Slow it right down

There are so many reasons to start speaking more slowly, starting today.

Speak slowly and you'll be giving yourself more time to construct sentences in your head, meaning you have less chance of stumbling over your words.

Speak more slowly and you will sound like an expert, considered and thoughtful, and you'll get the attention of the people around you who will hang on your every word.

Speak slowly and people will listen intently and your confidence will rise immediately.

Oh, and remember to breathe and smile a lot!

115   Eureka!

The late UK prime minister Margaret Thatcher thought that sleep was a waste of valuable time – she is reputed to have slept for only four hours each night. What she maybe didn't realise was that during sleep your brain is busy repairing itself and consolidating memories. You can't concentrate with a tired, stressed and frazzled brain. The average person needs around eight hours' sleep per day – the equivalent of spending a third of your life asleep.

Sleep deficit creates fatigue, drowsiness, gloomy moods and impaired decision making, reduced creativity, reckless behaviour and paranoia. Healthy sleep must contain rapid eye movement (REM) periods – times when you dream – dreams aid your creativity. During your dreams your brain is making sense of the world, discovering new links and associations between existing memories, looking for patterns, formulating rules and even solving problems.

You may even have a 'Eureka!' moment after waking up from a power nap of 20 minutes in the afternoon to maintain your productivity.

116   Skills acquisition

Your ability to acquire new skills plays an important part in building your resilience as it helps to develop a sense of mastery and competency – both of which can be utilised during challenging times – as well as increasing your self-esteem and ability to problem solve.

The skills you learn will depend on your personality. Some people might benefit from improving cognitive skills like 'working memory' or 'selective attention', which will help with everyday functioning. Others might benefit from learning new activities through competency-based learning.

Acquiring new skills within a group setting works well because it has the added benefit of offering social support, which also cultivates resilience. What new skill can you start to acquire?

117   Develop quiet confidence

Confidence is believing you're good. It's a feeling of self-assurance that comes from an appreciation of your abilities or qualities. Arrogance is believing you're better than anyone else, or having an exaggerated sense of your importance or abilities. Importantly, arrogance often masks insecurity, which is why arrogant people are boastful about their achievements and abilities while tending to demean others.

Your confidence stems from true self-worth – a genuine belief and pride in your achievements and abilities. Confident self-assuredness contributes to your inner calm, helping you show composure, willingness to listen, ability to learn and keenness to help others.

118   Set a course

Setting a goal is your ability to create a plan of action that allows you to choose where you want to go and what you want to achieve in life. Your goal will give you long-term vision and short-term motivation. Setting goals allows you to know where you need to focus your energy, what you need to move towards and what you need to move away from.

With a goal, you know if you're making progress, and progress encourages you to keep going. The more skilled you are at creating a specific goal, the better the chance you will have of achieving it. Goal setting will improve your performance because it increases your motivation and improves your skill acquisition and your self-confidence, which assures you that you are headed in the right direction.

119   Seek support

The best thing you can do to build your resilience is to seek support. Building relationships that create love, care and trust, provide role models, and offer encouragement and reassurance will help to bolster your resilience.

You will experience setbacks and difficult emotions, but you can tap into your strengths and the strengths of others to overcome every challenge you face.

120   Take advice from your future self

Without a clear goal, it's hard to sustain your sense of motivation or hope. Without a clear goal, you can't have a meaningful identity. Start to see yourself as the person who has already achieved your goal. That doesn't mean you pretend to be that person today. But it does mean that you are consistently taking that person's advice – that of your 'future self'.

Start taking your future self's advice and make decisions based on your future self's preferences and circumstances, not your current ones. The more you think of yourself in the present, the more you stunt your potential. Your future self is far more important than your current self. Your current self is temporary and you need only hold on to it loosely. Decide who you want to be in the future.

The biggest regret most people have on their deathbed is that they didn't have the courage to be the person they wanted to be. Instead, they lived up to the expectations of those around them.

CHAPTER 5

DON'T FEAR THE FOCUS

121 The story of the lion, the donkey and the fox

A lion, a fox and a donkey were hunting together. They all gathered a huge amount of food and then had to decide how to divide it. The lion asked the donkey to divide the food. So the donkey chose to divide the portions equally. This made the lion, the king of beasts, angry and with his paw he killed the donkey. The lion then asked the fox to divide the food. The fox wasted no time. He quickly gave a huge heap to the lion and kept only a small portion for himself. The lion asked the fox, 'Who taught you to divide so fairly?' The fox replied, 'I learned from the donkey.'

The Lesson: Learn from the misfortunes of others. Failure in life is fine as long as you learn from it. Look at the mistakes other people have made and take note. It's always important to reflect on what you could have done better or what steps you could avoid in the future.

122 See what they see

Whether you want to admit it or not, we can all be a bit judgemental. Right now, people will view you in a certain way and have a preconceived idea of what you're capable of. That's because they've become accustomed to seeing you operate in your comfort zone.

But once you move out of your comfort zone, you'll prove to everyone that you're capable of much more than you've shown in the past. The increased confidence other people place in you as a result will bring about more opportunities than ever before.

123 Search for solutions

If you are able to come up with solutions to a problem, you'll be better able to cope with any problems that occur in your life.

Whenever you encounter a new challenge, make a quick list of some of the potential ways you could solve the problem. Get all your ideas out of your head onto paper. Start to experiment with different strategies and focus on developing a logical way to work through the issues you're facing.

By practising your problem-solving skills on a regular basis, you will be better prepared to cope when a serious challenge emerges.

124   Room for improvement

List three recent failures. They can be big or small, consequential or insignificant.

Include any relevant details about how you responded in each case. Did you wallow in self-recrimination? Did you berate yourself for an adequate performance or misguided decision?

Write down how you could have responded in a more positive manner. What could you have done better?

When you're finished, you'll notice a few fundamental differences in the way you could react to failure. This exercise reveals failures to be merely feedback rather than a final verdict on your capacity to perform.

125   No place for self-pity

Feeling sorry for yourself is exhausting and it takes a lot of energy. Self-pity also sabotages your commitment, making you more likely to resign yourself to failure rather than persevering through difficult situations.

In a state of self-pity, you'll end up dwelling on your unfavourable circumstances rather than focusing your mind to see your way through them. This affects your behaviour – instead of rolling up your sleeves and digging your heels in, you find yourself focusing on the fact that everything is going wrong. You wallow in negativity, which prevents you from taking the necessary action to overcome your adverse conditions. Self-pity is the bane of your psychological resilience.

126   Embrace the upside of failure

Taking risks gives you valuable experience as well as an opportunity to enjoy a specific reward. But when you take a risk, it exposes you to the possibility of failure. That can be an unsettling feeling. However, failure is nothing to fear. When there's some risk in play, there's almost always a price to pay, but it is seldom ruinous.

Start to adjust how you think about failure. Rather than perceiving it to be something to avoid at all costs, embrace the upside and the valuable insights and lessons you stand to gain. From every failure you learn more about what works and what doesn't.

So look for the small risks you can take every day.

127   Practise deliberately

I have fought twice in the boxing ring and it was a rapid and intense development of my mental toughness. A fighter knows that every fight – win or lose – will always improve their character. A fighter will never leave anything to luck and will always give 100 per cent during training.

The intensive training is deliberate – purposeful and systematic. While regular practice might include mindless repetitions, *deliberate* practice requires focused attention and is conducted with the specific goal of improving performance.

You need to be in the exact right frame of mind for every challenge you face.

128   Rest and recover

How often do you let your phone run out of battery? If you're anything like me, your phone will always be charged up and you never go anywhere without a charger.

You wouldn't let your phone's battery get low, so don't allow yourself to run on empty either. Your self-care is a priority, not a luxury. Rest promotes good mental health, boosts creativity, increases productivity, promotes wellbeing, reduces stress, improves mood and strengthens relationships. What's not to love about rest? Adequate rest helps your body activate inner healing so it can repair and recover.

Olympic athletes don't train all day, every day – they build in rest so they're in the best possible shape to compete. You need rest, just like they do.

129   Fear is in your mind

Fear is an emotion that will stand in the way of the development of your mental toughness. But remember that fear is only in your mind. It's a concept, not an object you can hold in your hand.

You're built to adapt to and deal with anything, so use every experience you have as a tool to help you rationalise your fears, learn more about yourself and focus clearly on what you really want.

When you're mentally tougher, fear is rendered powerless.

130   One step at a time

Crisis situations are daunting. Some challenges may even seem insurmountable. Resilient people are able to view these situations in a realistic way and set reasonable goals to deal with the problem.

When you find yourself becoming overwhelmed by a situation, take a step back to assess what is before you. Zoom out and see the bigger picture. Identify, and write down, all the possible solutions, scenarios and possibilities, then break them down into manageable steps. Take one step at a time to build your resilience and courage.

131   Remove temptation

There are no secrets to developing discipline – it requires time and effort, just like building any habit. And like building any habit, you can expect failure and frustration to be part of the process.

Be aware of this from the outset because you will stumble on occasions. You're not a robot, after all. You'll find it easier to resist temptations when you remove them from your environment. If you have difficulty resisting junk food, then just get rid of all the junk food in your house. Access stimulates your impulses. Lack of access helps you to control them.

132   Perfectly imperfect

Most of us would probably like to be perfect but we're willing to admit that we fall a little short. Some people are OK with that; some find it hard. The problem with perfectionism is that it is the scourge of mental toughness. Nothing breeds inaction and erodes your resilience as completely as the nagging thought that your performance might be anything less than perfect. To a perfectionist, that would be completely unacceptable.

This self-sabotage is a breeding ground for self-doubt, so throw away the concept of perfectionism. It is your imperfections that make you just perfect the way you are.

133   Refuse to quit

Focus your attention on what you need to do to accomplish your goal. Persistent people never take their eye off the ball and are determined to succeed, despite repeated setbacks, obstacles and failures. They're not afraid to make mistakes; they learn from them, never lose heart and keep going against all the odds. Giving up halfway through is not an option. Winners are not quitters.

Abraham Lincoln is always linked to determination and perseverance in the face of adversity and difficulty. He lost eight elections before becoming US president. He refused to quit. He was capable of great physical and mental discipline. His mind and body were in perfect harmony.

134   The story of the lion and the mouse

A lion was fast asleep until a mouse woke him up. The lion opened his big jaws to swallow the mouse. But the mouse begged the lion to think again, telling him he might be useful in the future. The lion laughed the idea off and let the mouse go.

Some time later, the lion was caught in a trap by some hunters. At that moment the same little mouse walked by and noticed the lion. He walked up to the trap and chewed the rope to free the lion. The mouse smiled and said, 'Was I not right?'

The Lesson: Little friends may prove to be great friends. You never know who will prove to be useful in the future. It's best to maintain great relationships with everyone and to be kind to all. You never know where your kindness could lead you.

135   Reframe

Your ability to develop mental toughness depends on how you think about your circumstances. If you perceive adversity and misfortune to be hardships and yourself a powerless victim, you'll be more inclined to lose heart and surrender. But if you perceive these setbacks as learning opportunities, you're more likely to see the positives in them.

Start to reframe how you interpret the challenging scenarios you face.

136   Find your ikigai

The Japanese have a term, *ikigai*, which translates as 'a reason for being'. This is anything that gives a deep sense of purpose to your life and makes it worthwhile. It is what you get up for every morning. Knowing your purpose helps you live life with integrity.

When you know your purpose in life, you'll fully understand who you are, what you are and why you are. And when you know yourself, it becomes easier to live a life that's true to your core values.

What's your purpose?

137   Reflect to learn

People who lack focus are unable to reflect and learn from past mistakes. They find it difficult to visualise and plan for the future.

Reflection is possibly your greatest source of learning, as you become aware of your own thinking processes. Learn how to organise your day so that you can spend time thinking, reflecting and planning. As you develop your skills, you can review their effectiveness. Take a step back to think about how you could do things better and work more carefully, safely and effectively.

You will need sustained, focused attention to improve your future performance. Even the most successful people could not achieve much if they lacked focus, reflection, determination and effort.

138   The road to happiness

'There is only one way to happiness and that is to cease worrying about things which are beyond the power of your will.' Epictetus

139   Power hit

Visualisation is the process where you create pictures and images in your mind of what you want to accomplish. It's a natural skill that people use all the time and you can learn to improve your visualisation abilities in order to raise your performance.

Visualisation is an invaluable tool that high performers in all walks of life use to achieve their goals. It can also help you to prepare for situations where you might normally get distracted or lose your focus or confidence.

Seeing or sensing images and movies in your mind allows your subconscious to begin preparing for the actual event. It's really powerful.

140   Pick yourself up

Fear is probably the most likely thing to prevent you from taking action. And failure is the thing that you intuitively fear the most.

You might shudder at the possibility that you'll do something that will have a negative outcome. You might worry that you'll make a fool of yourself and people will mock you. This is the reason it can be so difficult to venture outside your comfort zone. The upside of regularly failing and picking yourself up afterwards is that you slowly become desensitised to negative outcomes. You learn that negative outcomes are less consequential than you imagined them to be. You come to realise that your fears are overblown.

Grow accustomed to failure – see it as an opportunity to learn and improve.

What are you scared of?

141   Own it

Take responsibility for your actions. Even if there are others involved, own your part of it and don't blame anyone else. Be accountable for your actions and what led to this failure or setback. You are responsible for your choices, good or bad, no matter what anyone else does or what their part in it may have been.

If you don't take responsibility, you'll be less likely to succeed in making significant changes in your life. So own it and take responsibility.

142   Others first

Having self-awareness is great and necessary for building mental toughness. But doing something that benefits others more than yourself feels amazing.

Research shows that people who have a clear sense of purpose and are grateful for the life they are living often contribute more to the world beyond themselves than those who do not have this sense of gratitude. If you can see how other people benefit from your life, you'll feel more motivated to give back to humanity.

Engage in altruistic behaviours (like volunteering or donating money) to deepen your sense of purpose and increase the feeling of making a difference in the world.

143   Panning for gold

If you were able to turn every challenge you face into an opportunity, what would happen? Start to visualise how things could be if setbacks worked for you rather than against you.

Whatever challenge you are facing right now – either personal or professional – spend some time flipping it all on its head. Mind-map the options, realities and possibilities.

Somewhere deep inside this challenge there is a nugget of gold lying there waiting for you to pick it up and run with it.

144   Open up new limits

Any doubts you have in yourself will be deeply connected to the opinion you hold of yourself and the experiences you've had in your life so far. As much as 90 per cent of what you do as an adult has been dictated by subconscious patterns you learned as a child.

'Self-limiting beliefs' are the ones that have the most potential to impact negatively on you achieving your full potential. It's time to replace any self-limiting beliefs you hold with more empowering ones. Start this process today by examining your self-talk, the words you use when you speak to yourself. Are you mean or kind to yourself? Would you speak to your friends the way you speak to yourself?

Replace any unkind self-talk with the caring, sensitive, empathetic, kind words you would use for your best friend.

145   One thing at a time (part 1)

Multitasking is often worn as a badge of honour, but it is not healthy or productive. Multitasking significantly reduces your efficiency and performance because you can only give your full attention to one thing at a time.

When you try to do two (or more) things at once, your brain lacks the capacity to perform both tasks successfully. You're actually switching between individual tasks in rapid succession, which makes you less efficient and more likely to make mistakes.

Do one thing at a time. Do that thing well, with your full attention.

146   One thing at a time (part 2)

Despite conventional wisdom, multitasking slows you down. When you divide your attention it means you actually introduce distraction and increase the likelihood of mistakes. Technically, you can multitask – you can listen to the radio and do the ironing at the same time – but your mind can only completely focus and concentrate on one thing or thought at a time. Attempt many tasks at a time and you'll be more likely to miss important information and less likely to retain information, which will impair your problem solving, decision making and creativity.

Attempt one thing at time and give that one thing the attention it deserves.

147   Observe your thoughts

Try a meditation technique called 'observing thoughts' that will teach you to become the witness to your own thoughts, distancing you from the emotional attachments and judgements that influence your behaviour. This technique retrains your body to not become so emotionally charged by thoughts. Instead, you will simply observe the thoughts inside your mind, reduce mind chatter and induce calming emotions.

Start by taking a few gentle deep breaths in a quiet space, then shift your attention to the process of thinking. Notice each thought come and go like clouds floating through the sky. Observe your thoughts as if they are visitors passing in and out of a room.

148   No need for approval

When you seek approval from others, it hurts your self-confidence. It trains your mind to distrust your motivation and abilities. Instead, your mind learns to avoid taking action until it receives permission to do so from someone else. Over time you become wary and begin to harbour misgivings about your ability to perform.

It's important to recognise that you possess unique value. Your knowledge, skills, talents and adaptability eliminate the need for external validation – as long as your confidence levels are aligned with reality. You can be self-assured and self-assertive when you face uncertainty.

149   Take down the facade

Understanding your reason for being allows you to live a life with integrity. Know your purpose in life and you'll understand who you are and what you are here for. You will feel more satisfied in general because you'll be living true to your core values.

When this is the case, you won't have to put on a facade or act as though you are passionate about anything you truly dislike. Instead, your passion for everything you do will be genuine and you will always show up as your true, authentic self.

Think about your core values and what gets you really excited about life.

150   No adversity, no growth

Be compassionate with yourself and realise all the ways adversity has made you strong. People who face difficulties and adversity inevitably become stronger. No adversity, no growth.

Of course, it depends on a lot of other factors – the scale of the adversity, the level of support available – but by learning to cope with stress and having that experience, you gain confidence and you gain preparation. You see how you're broken rather than how you're strong.

Focus on the resilience and see yourself as someone who is even better prepared for life than the average person because you've already lived so much of it.

CHAPTER 6

TAKE A VIEW

151   The story of the hare and the tortoise

A hare was boasting about his speed in front of the other animals and challenged any one of them to race him. A tortoise accepted his challenge. At first the hare thought it was a joke, but the tortoise was being serious. So, soon after, they began the race.

The hare ran full speed ahead, and to make fun of the tortoise, he decided to take a nap. The tortoise kept slowly going and going. When the hare woke up, he noticed that the tortoise was near the finishing post and run as he might, the hare failed to win the race.

The Lesson: Slow and steady wins the race. Sometimes in life, it might look like other people are racing ahead of you. But you never know what obstacle could stop them in their tracks. It's important to keep moving forward and one day you will get there.

152   New tricks

Acquiring new skills plays an important part in building resilience because it helps to develop a sense of mastery and competency. You can use this sense of mastery during challenging times as well as to increase your self-esteem and your ability to solve problems.

You might find that you benefit from boosting cognitive skills such as improving your memory or developing selective attention. Or you might benefit from learning a new hobby or activity. Whichever way feels most useful to you, acquiring any new skills will cultivate your resilience and mental toughness.

What new skill can you acquire that will increase your motivation and energy?

153   Little by little

How often do you face a fear that provokes anxiety in you? A well-used technique to conquer the fears you face (used a lot in cognitive behavioural therapy) is 'controlled exposure', which refers to the gradual exposure to anxiety-provoking situations. It can help you to overcome your fears.

This approach can foster resilience, and especially so when it also involves acquiring a new skill. Public speaking, for example, is a useful life skill but also something that evokes fear in many people. Like most, I used to be terrified of public speaking, but I set myself small goals involving controlled exposure to develop my ability and confidence. I spoke to small audiences at first and progressively faced larger audiences. I now speak regularly to hundreds and thousands of people without any anxiety.

What can you expose yourself to gradually that would help you to your fear?

154   Find your light-bulb moment

The inventor Thomas Edison was intimately acquainted with failure. He invented the light bulb in 1878 after thousands of failed attempts. Regarding the experience, Edison said: 'I haven't failed. I've just found 10,000 ways that won't work.'

He understood that persistence in the face of failure is critical to ultimate success. Your refusal to give up is more important than your intelligence, talent or skill. It is your mental toughness that will play a bigger part than anything else in your success.

155   Mix it up

When you're living inside of your comfort zone, the bulk of your actions are habitual: automatic, subconscious and requiring limited focus. But when you move out of your comfort zone, you no longer rely on those habitual responses. You're forced to concentrate and focus on the new action in a way you never do in your comfort zone.

The more things you can do in new ways, with new approaches, the more you will develop your mental toughness.

156   Look up and look around

As you get older, you see less and less of what's really going on around you. You create quick references to things and file them away in your brain as 'familiar'. Slow down and start to observe the faces of the people that pass by. Look up at the buildings and notice tiny details that surround you. Consider the beauty you see. Smell the air and touch the plants.

This is a beautifully simple exercise because it shifts something significant inside you.

157   Never. Give. Up

Your tenacity is your fierce blend of perseverance, determination, persistence and grit. These traits of mental toughness determine how successful and happy your life will be.

Think about any successful person, in any avenue of life, and you will realise that the ones that rise to the top are not the most talented or skilful but the ones who never, ever give up in pursuit of their dream.

Which successful people do you admire? What traits would you like to adopt from these people? Set your goal. Commit fully. But most importantly… Never. Give. Up.

158   Lift your mood naturally

Endorphins are natural chemicals that your body releases to help to regulate your mood and improve your ability to cope. When you can promote the production of endorphins, you'll feel more focused, more emotionally stable, happier and calmer.

Physical exercise is the best way to encourage endorphins, but other ways you can try today are by simply giving, laughing, listening to music and having a romantic evening in.

Which appeals to you most?

159   Real or imagined?

Your subconscious mind believes everything you tell it, without question. Your subconscious mind will file negative and positive inputs equally, believing that everything is accurate and valuable information, whether it is or not. What's locked into your subconscious goes in as if it's actually happened – your conscious mind cannot tell the difference between what is real and what you have imagined.

We don't always become aware of our intuitions immediately, as they often depend on a complicated interaction between the unconscious and the conscious mind. Sometimes you might sense a vague edge of an idea that feels compelling and work on it both above and below awareness before a clear insight evolves. Achieving consistency in the conscious mind takes mental discipline. The mental discipline you develop will increase your performance and make you more likely to achieve your goals.

160   Long-term view

They say that the only thing constant in life is change. Most people hate change, preferring routine and predictability. Wouldn't it be helpful if you could accept that change is simply part of living?

As a result of changes or difficult circumstances, certain goals you have may no longer be realistic or attainable. Accepting what you cannot change allows you to focus on the things that you do have control, or influence, over.

Looking ahead and taking a longer-term view, you'll be better able to deal with what's happened and accept it as something that had to happen for you to move forward.

What can you influence today to make tomorrow better?

161   Name that emotion

It's sometimes hard to put a name to your feelings. It might even be tough to admit to yourself when you're nervous or sad. But labelling your emotions can take a lot of the sting out of them. So check in with yourself a few times a day and ask yourself how you're feeling. Set alarms on your phone for morning, afternoon and evening. If you can put a name to the emotion, or the mix of emotions, you'll feel stronger.

Take notes on your phone or write them down. You can use an emotions word list to help you identify what you're feeling, too. It's important to connect with how you feel or you won't know how your feelings affect your decisions. When you're angry or embarrassed, you may take big risks you don't need to.

162   Motivation in all its forms

Four different types of motivation will drive you through the tough times, making you perform at a higher level, maintaining your focus on your commitments. They are:

1. Extrinsic – motivation that is driven from an external source, like a prize or reward

2. Intrinsic – the motivation that comes from within yourself and occurs as a result of your actions aligning with your values, like your boss saying you've done a great job

3. Introjected – an internalised motivation but in a negative form, when you do something to maintain self-esteem to avoid guilt

4. Identified – a form of motivation that happens when you feel the need to perform a task but you don't act on it.

Getting a grasp of these different forms of motivation will help you to achieve your goals.

What kind of motivation are you experiencing today?

163   Monitor the changes

When you're developing your mental toughness, it is important for you to know whether all the changes you're making are actually making a difference. Technology and gadgets can help you to keep an eye on how well you're dealing with the situations you face. Use a blood pressure monitor to track your blood pressure because, if it is raised, you could be at risk of a heart attack or stroke. You can reduce your blood pressure by being physical active, eating a healthy, balanced diet and cutting down on alcohol and salt.

164   Mistakes need mindfulness

Mistakes can haunt you. Long after the dust has settled, you might replay an incident over and over, ruminating on what you could have done differently, analysing each detail as a reflection of your shortcomings.

This pattern of thought is not only counterproductive, it's bad for your mental health. Excessive self-criticism can contribute to feelings of depression and anxiety, so use mindfulness to bring yourself into the present moment. Take in every sensation of where you are and what you are doing right now.

It is the antithesis of recalling painful memories. Every time your mind wanders to that mistake, focus on your current situation.

165   Mind the gap

If you were given the chance to teach others, what would you teach them? Think about what you would change about the world and what knowledge you want to pass on to future generations. This question also forces you to reflect on the things in life that you believe you are competent in and able to teach other people about.

How would you want to improve other people's lives, or where do you believe there is a gap in knowledge that you could fill?

166   One thought at a time

You can only have one thought at a time. You can only think of one thing at a time. I'm sure it often feels as though you're thinking of more than one thing because your thoughts are coming in such rapid-fire succession, but the reality is that only one thought can be represented at a time. Only when that thought moves out and clears the space can you make way for another thought.

Your thoughts can only be generated from one of three places: the past, the present or the future. Your body is always in the present. It is impossible for it to physically function in the past or the future. When your mind and body are in the same place and concentrating on the same thing, you will get the best results. Your highest degree of accomplishment will occur when your mind and body are in the present.

167 Make time for your wellness

Warning: if you don't make time for your wellness, you will be forced to make time for your illness.

You might want to read that again.

The truth is, you're always going to be busy and pulled in many directions, so living a healthy lifestyle can be challenging. But it is also true that prioritising quality fitness and relaxation time for yourself will help you to stay physically and mentally healthy, and well. Set yourself a daily routine of exercise that is achievable and fits into your day. You have far more time available to you than you have been telling yourself.

When you begin to feel the benefits (which will be immediate), you can start to extend this time to build in new activities and regimes.

168 Make the invisible visible

An amateur and a professional sportsperson might have very similar skills or abilities. Often, the reason why amateurs don't turn professional is because they crack under the pressure of a competition. They simply can't cope with the stress.

The ability to cope with, or manage, stress and pressure is a quality of the mentally tough. So, ultimately, it is your mental responses to situations that determine your success. If you can develop the ability to manage whatever is going on around you, you will enjoy a more relaxed, successful and happy life.

Start to make the invisible visible! Today, when faced with a challenge or setback, write down your mental response to the situation. What went through your mind and what happened? How can you change your mental response to get a better outcome?

169   Look in the mirror with kindness

It's time to remove the 'I want you to like me' sticker from your forehead and place it on the mirror where it belongs.

You know the old adage that you can't expect anyone to love you until you love yourself? It's true, because self-love is a state of appreciation for yourself that grows from actions that support your physical, psychological and spiritual growth. Self-love means having a high regard for your own wellbeing and happiness. Self-love means taking care of your own needs and not sacrificing your wellbeing to please others.

So take a long, hard look in the mirror and acknowledge the great things about you. Make a list of your best qualities. You'll find yourself respecting your body – eating better and moving your body more – because you'll realise your mental wellbeing is just as important as your physical wellbeing.

170   Reflect on the future

A technique that can help you better handle stress involves thinking about the outcomes of stressful events in the relatively far future. For example, you might tell yourself that 'time heals all wounds' or 'this will soon pass'.

The ability to think about a future where you will no longer be feeling so bad about whatever you're struggling with can help you get through difficult experiences. It can reduce the intensity of negative emotions and the distress caused by the situation.

So next time you are in the midst of a stressful situation, try to look back at the situation from some time in the future. Start today by recalling a recent stressful event. Choose something very specific and imagine how important this moment will be five years after this event.

Practise this technique regularly to reduce feelings of stress.

171   Never stop trying

Don't give up. You have no idea how close to success you actually are. Keep trying, keep pushing, keep working hard every day and you will have a much higher chance of succeeding.

Don't give up because, if you do, you'll have no chance of succeeding.

172   Look after yourself

When you're stressed, it can be all too easy to neglect your own needs. Losing your appetite, ignoring exercise and not getting enough sleep are all common reactions to a crisis situation. Focus on building your skills of self-care, even when you are feeling troubled. Make time for activities that you enjoy.

By taking care of your own needs, you can boost your overall health and resilience and be fully ready to face life's challenges.

Avoid using alcohol, nicotine or caffeine as a coping mechanism. These faulty responses will just add to your problems. Caffeine and nicotine are stimulants – too much of them and the body reacts, causing anxiety. Alcohol is a depressant.

Alongside holidays, taking even a short 15-minute break at work to relax and recharge your batteries will power your coping strategy.

173   Listen deeply

Listen with intent. Don't ask questions and then not listen to the answer. It makes the person you're talking to feel as though their opinions have been voiced and then totally disregarded. After a while, they won't contribute at all. They won't trust that you'll listen.

When you're in a conversation, seriously regard what the other person has to say, consider it, listen deeply. People will engage with you and start to trust you if they feel you're truly listening.

During your next conversation, consider what you could say that would add value. Don't be afraid of silence because it doesn't always have to be filled. Silence offers you an opportunity to listen and consider your response.

174   Mistakes live in the past

Your mistakes do not exist in the present. It's only after you've done something that didn't turn out the way you wanted that you decide that you've made a mistake and so it *becomes* a mistake. Mistakes are related to your expected outcomes.

From now on, when things don't quite go your way, look back and understand what you might have done differently so that next time you have the benefit of that experience.

175   Get below the surface

A poor listener is unable to separate their own needs and interests from those of others. Everything they hear comes with an automatic bias: how does this affect me?

Poor listeners are more likely to interrupt – either they have already jumped to conclusions about what someone is saying or it's just of no interest to them. Be a good listener by being open-minded, giving genuinely interested attention to others and allowing yourself the time and space to fully absorb what they say. Deep listening seeks not just the surface meaning but where the speaker is coming from – what purpose, interest or need is motivating their speech. Good listening encourages others to feel heard and to speak more openly and honestly. Be a deep listener in the next conversation you have today.

176   Lighten your load

Maintain resilience in the face of negative pressures by developing your capacity to deal with stressful situations. This is a basic foundation for building your mental toughness. When your stress level exceeds your ability to cope, you need to restore the balance by reducing the stressors, increasing your ability to cope, or both.

Today, make a list of all the things you'd like to achieve in the next few days or weeks. Prioritise this list, putting the most important at the top. Now make a list of anything that feels overwhelming or is likely to trigger stress in you. Prioritise what is most important to achieve first (which may be the hardest thing!). Plan ahead, change your surroundings and reap the benefits of a lighter load.

177   Learn from tough times

Look for opportunities for self-discovery. Sometimes tragedy can result in great learnings and personal growth. Living through a difficult situation can increase your self-confidence and your sense of self-worth, strengthen your relationships and teach you a great deal about yourself. You will almost certainly experience hardship, but along with that you'll start to enjoy a heightened appreciation for life and deeper spirituality.

178   Be mindful of your mood

Mindfulness is a great way to calm your body and mind, as well as helping you deal with issues that may be causing your low mood. By meditating and focusing on your thoughts, feelings and sensations in your body and in the world around you, you can really improve your mental wellbeing.

Mindfulness can give you a new sense of calm and help you to process any negative emotions. Try keeping a mood diary to help you track changes in your mood – it will reveal the activities, places or people that make you feel better or worse. It can help you appreciate the positive parts of your day and reveal what could be triggering your low mood.

179   Let yourself be drawn

Simply waiting for a problem to go away on its own only prolongs the crisis. Instead, you can try to resolve the issue immediately. While there may not be any fast or simple solution to making your situation better and less stressful, start by being super clear about what the problem actually is.

Define the problem by writing it down in one short sentence. Remember that yours isn't the only view – everyone will have a different perspective on the same issue. Generate multiple solutions and options and evaluate alternatives. Listen to your intuition as it draws you to one of your options.

180   Do what you say you're going to do

When you do what you have said you'll do, people see you as a responsible and reliable person. This is admirable, and useful, as many people won't want to deal with you if you're irresponsible. People give their trust to friends they can count on and give their business to companies they admire.

A responsible person is one who can be trusted because they are accountable for their behaviour. Being trusted is a good feeling we all enjoy. This feeling of trust will boost your self-esteem and self-worth.

As a responsible person, you tackle the difficult tasks without blaming others for setbacks or problems. You are responsible for your successes and failures, and along with any risk come great rewards.

CHAPTER 7

TIME TO BE YOURSELF

181   The story of the gnat and the bull

A gnat settled down on a bull's horn. After a while he decided to fly off. Before leaving, he asked the bull if it was OK for him to go. The bull hadn't even noticed the gnat, so he replied, 'I did not know you had come, and I shall not miss you when you go away.'

The Lesson: Some people are of more consequence in their own eyes than in the eyes of those around them. This doesn't mean that you are insignificant, but sometimes the things you do and say won't have the impact you anticipate. It's important to be yourself and not to expect everyone to notice your presence.

182   Lean on me

You can strengthen your resilience today by building connections to your family, friends and community.

You probably underestimate the importance of building healthy relationships with people who care about you, who will listen to your problems and who can offer support during difficult times. Empathetic, understanding people can help you to reclaim hope and remind you that you're never alone in this world. Likewise, assisting others in their time of need can benefit you greatly and foster your sense of resilience.

Who can you lean on today? And who can you offer support and help to?

183   Flex your mindset

Your resilient mindset will be a flexible mindset. As you encounter stressful circumstances and events in your life, it's helpful to maintain flexibility and balance in a number of ways.

Let yourself experience strong emotions and realise when you may need to put them aside in order to continue functioning.

Step forward and take action to deal with your problems and meet the demands of daily living, but also know when to step back and rest/re-energise.

Spend time with loved ones who offer support and encouragement; nurture yourself.

Rely on others, but also know when to rely on yourself.

184   Journal it

When you write down your feelings and the responses they trigger, it helps you to uncover any disruptive patterns. Sometimes, it's enough to mentally trace emotions back through your thoughts. Putting feelings onto paper can allow you to reflect on them more deeply. It also helps you to recognise when specific circumstances, like trouble at work or family conflict, contribute to 'harder-to-control emotions'.

Identifying specific triggers makes it possible to come up with ways to manage them more productively. You may find that journalling brings you the most benefit when you do it daily. Keep a journal of your feelings and jot down intense emotions as they happen. Try to note the triggers and your reaction. If your reaction didn't help, use your journal to explore more helpful possibilities for the future.

185   Laugh at it all

Resilient people live meaningful lives. They love to laugh and have a positive and hopeful attitude to life. They don't take themselves too seriously and they have a sense of humour about life's challenges. For resilient people, happiness comes because they believe in who they are, they know what they are doing and they love what they do.

Resilient people are optimistic and believe in their own strength and ability to overcome problems. In a crisis, a resilient person will be positive, open and willing to find the solution. They will not dwell on the problem but look forward to the future with possible solutions to their problems.

Laughter, positivity and hope are important strategies when you want to build resilience in your life.

186   Nurture your social network

Develop a strong social network by having caring, supportive people around you who can act as a protective barrier during times of setbacks or crisis. It is important to have people you can confide in, whom you trust and admire.

While simply talking about a situation with a friend or loved one will not make troubles go away, it allows you to share your feelings, gain support, receive positive feedback and come up with possible solutions to your problems. The activities you engage in with your friends help you to calm down, relax and have a laugh. And let's not forget how important a good laugh is to our physiology – laughing boosts the immune system that may be depleted during stress.

And worry not, you can learn to embrace the absurdity of life at any age – it's never too late!

187   Become the focus of your attention

Don't confuse self-awareness with consciousness. Your consciousness is your awareness of your body, environment and lifestyle. Self-awareness is the understanding you have of yourself, as a unique individual. It's about you becoming aware of your traits, behaviours and feelings, and how they align (or not) with your values and standards. It's actually a psychological state in which you become the focus of your attention.

When you develop your self-awareness, you'll be able to more easily recognise what you do well and what you can improve. You'll start to feel more happiness because your ideals and values will start to align with your actions.

What can you discover about yourself today that you've never noticed before?

188   Kick-start your motivation

If you're feeling a little stuck, losing motivation or unable to accomplish your goals, be kind to yourself and follow this simple idea for getting back on track.

Take a giant step back. Zoom out because it's time to reprioritise. Ask yourself, what is really the most important thing you want to achieve? What matters the most to you? Focus on this one thing and create a new list of smaller steps that move you towards this goal. Don't set any more goals until you have completed these smaller steps.

Remind yourself what you're capable of, how much this matters to you and how good you will feel when you have reached the goal.

189   Keep your focus

Your concentration is your ability to stay focused on a certain activity and also your ability to refocus following a distraction.

Distractions are everywhere, and there's nothing wrong with distractions if you're able to manage them well. Learn to stay on target by reminding yourself what your primary focus is – what exactly you are trying to achieve. Reduce your load to maybe just two or three tasks for the day. Break those down into smaller parts and set about achieving each small step.

You'll find it much easier to avoid distractions when each small step is easily achievable.

190   The story of the donkey and the well

One day a farmer's donkey fell down a well. The animal cried piteously for hours as the farmer tried to figure out what to do. Finally, he decided the animal was old and the well needed to be covered up anyway – it just wasn't worth the trouble to retrieve the donkey.

The farmer invited all of his neighbours to come over and help him fill in the well. They all grabbed a shovel and began to throw dirt into the well. At first the donkey cried horribly, then, to everyone's amazement, he quietened down. A few shovel loads later, the farmer finally looked down and was astonished at what he saw.

With each shovel of dirt that hit his back, the donkey was doing something amazing. He would shake it off and take a step up. Before long, to everyone's amazement, the donkey stepped up over the edge of the well and happily trotted off.

The Lesson: Life is going to shovel dirt on you, all kinds of dirt. The trick to getting out of the well is to shake it off and take a step up. Each of your troubles is a stepping stone. You can get out of the deepest wells by not stopping, never giving up. Shake it off and take a step up.

191   It's all about you

You cannot be given a life by someone else. Of all the people you will know in your lifetime, you are the only one who will never leave.

You are the only answer to the problems in your life.

You are the biggest obstacle in your life.

You are the answer and the solution. To everything.

Read this again.

192   Keep it cold

Staying hydrated is vital for your health. Consuming two or three litres of water every day supports your body functions, including your digestion, metabolism, getting rid of waste, maintaining normal body temperature and keeping your organs healthy. There's been plenty of debate about whether it's better to drink warm or ice-cold water, but personally I say keep it cold. Cold water can prevent you from getting headaches, helps you to burn more calories during exercise and flushes out unwanted toxins from your body.

Cold water activates sensors just under your skin, which then increase your heart rate and add an adrenaline rush to give you a feeling of being 'alive'. Drinking ice-cold water helps you to stay attentive and more focused so that you can make better, quicker decisions. Often, people involved in accidents are given a glass of cold water to keep their mind alert and reduce sensations of pain.

Drink plenty of water every day, but keep it cold!

193   Keep an emotional distance

When you're struggling with a challenge, emotionally distance yourself from it. When you're able to view your experiences as if you were 'a fly on the wall' or as if you were someone else who is witnessing your experiences from afar, it can keep you from getting stuck in your negative emotions.

Emotional distancing also makes it less likely that you will replay the unpleasant details of the event, and as a result you may feel better when bad things happen. To practise this technique, first recall a recent stressful conflict you had with another person. Choose something very specific. Now reimagine the stressful event from an outside observer's viewpoint – from the point of view of a stranger on the street or a fly on the wall. Try to notice how being an outside observer helps make the experience seem less intense.

194   Just say yes

Your life is one big experiment, so the more you explore and try, the better. Say yes more often, even when you don't think you're ready. When you're working, say yes to new projects, new opportunities, new roles, even when you've not done them before.

Saying yes to new opportunities expands your knowledge and helps you to see things from a different perspective. When you say yes, your life becomes more fulfilling and you'll see positive changes creeping in.

Expand your horizons and explore more avenues of interest. Stretch your awareness of all the options available to you. Explore the possibilities of new places, events and ideas to help you define your future confidently. Say yes and who knows, you might find yourself enjoying something you never got the chance to do earlier.

195   Being brave is best

Being brave is better than simply having confidence because it means you are doing something – taking action. Brave action mean you are stretching yourself, pushing yourself, growing, learning and trying something new.

Having courage is necessary for you to lead an eventful, exciting life because fear will always be inescapable and only your braveness will conquer the fear in you.

Bravery is conquering your fear and moving ahead without letting anyone know that you are afraid. When fear makes you weak and directionless, bravery gives you the freedom to live life on your terms.

The bravest thing you can ever do in your life is to love and respect yourself. You will become free and start living your dreams once you start loving yourself. Does that sound scary?

196   Get into the creative flow

Writing stuff down is an act of self-care. Getting it all off your chest and on to a piece of paper helps you to improve your resilience. Not only is journalling helpful as a way of processing and releasing your emotions, it's also a way to document what is happening as it unfolds. By writing, you enter a flow of creativity, which can be a brilliant antidote to anxiety or depression. Absorb yourself in the process of writing and you momentarily step out of the trauma or stress around you and into a safe place of calm.

Grab some paper and write about how you feel right now. Write about a time when you overcame something similar. Write about how grateful you are for what you have.

197   Keep your motivation high

Motivation and hard work go hand in hand, but you might notice your motivation to work hard diminish if you aren't seeing any results. A lack of results can cause you to give up on your goal. It can also decrease your ability to stay focused and make you less productive.

It is important to remain optimistic. One of the benefits of hard work is that when you see progress and results, your motivation increases. As you start feeling more confident and your improvements become more apparent, you feel even more motivated and fulfilled.

Recognising your progress also makes you feel more encouraged to continue to work hard. When you have a feeling of unlimited potential, you must remember it was your hard work that got you there.

198   There are no limits

You are capable of doing anything you want. You have far more ability and resources than you give yourself credit for. Based on the information you already have in your head, you can use positive self-talk to override any negative information that you may have spinning around your mind.

With the information you have in your head, the way you talk to yourself and the way you respond, you will be able to choose how great your success will be.

199   It's all linked

There is a complete interdependency between your thoughts, your feelings and your behaviour. Your thoughts determine how you feel and your body reacts according to how you feel. If you want to find out why you are behaving the way you are, spend a moment tracking back to check out the thoughts you had that created the mood you're in and resulted in your behaviour.

200   The boring bit

Think of a skill you've mastered. Reflect for a moment on the time and attention you devoted to it. Think about how much you practised to get it right. There were undoubtedly times when you felt bored during the process. That's only natural as your brain is stimulated by new things and you're excited by the prospect of learning new skills and putting them to use. The trouble is, mastering a skill requires practice and repetition, and when you practise something over and over it starts to become boring.

Unfortunately, there's no way around it. You have to put in time to maintain your proficiency. Boredom is a precondition of mastery. No one masters anything without experiencing boredom in the process.

If you plan to master a new skill, then expect to get bored on the journey.

201   Keep it in perspective

It's easy to get overwhelmed by a situation and think that nothing else matters. A key to coping, and reminding yourself that challenging moments will pass, is to keep things in perspective. This means taking into consideration the true measure of importance of a situation, in a wise and reasonable way.

To keep a healthy perspective you need to step back from a situation and see it as a 'whole', with everything in proper proportion to everything else. Slow down your thinking and become aware of your own perspective. Then actively decide to use a different lens, zoom out, step back and see the bigger picture. Seeing things from a different perspective helps you to solve any problems more effectively.

202   Just breathe

You may notice that when you're stressed or anxious, your breathing changes. Your breaths get shorter and shallower. This has a knock-on effect to how your body and mind feel.

Take a few deep breaths to help slow your breathing and your heart rate. When you breathe deeply, it helps to calm your mind. Relax your shoulders, inhale through your nose and exhale slowly through your mouth. You can purse your lips slightly when you do this, but make sure your jaw stays relaxed.

You can repeat this deep breathing exercise as many times as you need to until you start to feel less stressed or anxious.

203   It's now that counts

Your future is determined by what you do and what you don't do in the present. Living in the moment can take quite a lot of practice, but by practising mindfulness you will reduce stress, boost your immune system and lower your blood pressure, among many other physical and mental benefits. Mindful people are generally more secure, have higher self-esteem and are happier.

Start to notice the world around you – the small things. Be thankful for them. Live for the moment. Live in the moment.

204   Daydream believer

Science is increasingly discovering the sophistication and value of our imagination. Daydreaming is both one of the most powerful tools you have and one of the most undervalued. Staring out the window at work doesn't look productive the way grinding away on your laptop does, but when it comes to creating innovative solutions, letting your mind wander is invaluable.

Imagine yourself doing something in the future and start to really feel as though it is true, as if it's actually happened. When you can do this, you can start to imagine how things will go your way and you'll become more likely to perform the same way in the real world.

Take some time every day to let your mind wander and imagine yourself performing at a high level. This will make you get stronger and you will perform in the same way in real life.

205   There's a time for feelings

If you're experiencing intense feelings, the best thing can be to keep some distance from them in order to make sure you're reacting to them in reasonable ways. This distance might be physical, like leaving an upsetting situation for example. But you can also create some mental distance by distracting yourself. While you don't want to block or avoid feelings entirely, it's not harmful to distract yourself until you're in a better place to deal with them. Just make sure you do come back to them – healthy distractions are only temporary. Try taking a walk, watching a funny film, spending a few minutes with your pet or talking to a loved one.

206   It's got to matter

Have you ever set a goal that was unimportant to you? Chances are you probably didn't take it seriously. It's easy to abandon unimportant goals at the first sign of difficulty. That's what happens when you don't feel a true sense of ownership for the things you set out to accomplish.

It's OK to abandon a goal when it no longer aligns with your long-term aspirations, but if you want to persevere when life gets tough, you must feel passionate about achieving the outcome. You must feel accountable for it. Set goals that matter.

207   Self-pity is a choice

People who habitually feel sorry for themselves often give up when they're confronted with challenges. It's important to recognise that self-pity is a choice. It's an attitude you adopt rather than one that overtakes you. Once you adopt a negative attitude, it can quickly gain a foothold in your mind, prompting you to instinctively blame your failures on your circumstances.

However, when you express gratitude, you underscore the fact that you possess resources, both internally and externally, that will help you to endure misfortune and hardships. When you voice your appreciation for your talents and abilities, you're evaluating your self-confidence while remaining open to experiencing further growth.

208   It's only feedback

You've no doubt heard the phrase: 'That which doesn't kill you makes you stronger.' It typically refers to tragedy, but it equally applies to failure. If you interpret failure simply as 'feedback', it toughens you up. Each incident further desensitises you to crippling emotions that might otherwise paralyse you.

As you learn from every setback you face, you will become steadily more courageous when you're faced with uncertainty. The idea of making the wrong decision or a mistake and consequently experiencing a negative outcome will hold less and less fear for you. Negative outcomes become nothing but useful, constructive feedback which presents you with an opportunity to learn and improve.

209 It's all about me, me, me

Developing your emotional intelligence begins with self-awareness. Focusing on yourself gives you the power of introspection so that you can connect with your authentic inner self, which will enable you to make better decisions. You need to trust your intuition or gut feelings, and not ignore something that feels right or wrong.

Becoming more self-aware will give you the power to influence outcomes. It will help you to become a better decision maker. Increased self-awareness will give you more self-confidence, and as a result you'll communicate with more clarity and intention. With increased self-awareness you will see and understand things from multiple perspectives. It will free you from assumptions and biases.

The first question you must ask yourself in order to develop self-awareness is: 'What am I really like to be around?'

210 The only constant is change

Avoid seeing the challenges and setbacks you face as insurmountable problems. You cannot change the external events happening around you, but you can control your reaction to these events. In your life there will always be challenges, but it's important to look beyond whatever stressful situation you are faced with and remember that circumstances will change.

The only constant is change. What is happening in your life today that you could react differently to? Take notice of the subtle ways in which you may already start feeling better as you deal with this difficult situation in a new way. Ask yourself: 'What am I really feeling here? What has happened to make me feel this way?' Then practise the art of changing your emotional response because when you control how you react, you will see a remarkable difference in the situation you are facing.

CHAPTER 8

THE GIFT OF GRIT

211   The story of the dog and the shadow

A dog was walking home with a piece of meat in his mouth. On his way, he crossed a river and looked into the water. He mistook his own reflection for another dog and wanted *his* meat also. But as he opened his mouth, the meat fell into the river and fell into the water and sank to the bottom of the river, out of reach.

The Lesson: It is foolish to be greedy. Everyone wants more! Of course, we always strive to be better and have bigger things. But it's important to reflect on the things you do have and not take them for granted. Because one day you might end up with nothing but regrets about things you could have done.

212   You are constantly growing

There is great value in performing 'self-evaluations' on a regular basis. You can do this in order to realign your confidence levels with reality.

Sit down every so often and reflect on how you've grown and consider the new skills you've learned. Think about peculiar situations in which you've found yourself and how you've handled them. Take stock of people you've recently met, conversations you've had with strangers and tasks you performed that were once unfamiliar to you.

You're constantly growing. It's all too easy to fail to recognise how much you've grown because it happens so gradually.

213   Love what you do

Motivation is easy when you absolutely love what you're doing. Your work fills a large part of your life, and the only way to be truly satisfied is to do great work. And the only way to do great work is to love what you do.

Doing what you love is an opportunity to experience what many people are lacking these days – consistent, genuine happiness on a daily basis.

No matter how motivated you are by money and status, you can't give 100 per cent of your time, effort, motivation, dedication and work ethic to a job or career that you don't love. You can't give your all if you don't feel a strong excitement or passion for what you're doing. It's just not possible.

Check with yourself: is your heart really in it?

214   True grit

'Come what may, all bad fortune is to be conquered by endurance.'
Virgil

215   Intimidation can be good

Before you can do something well, at some point you have to do it without any competence or knowledge about what you're doing. And in order to continue working at something even after you have made some mistakes and embarrassed yourself, you have to be passionate about it. These activities are meaningful enough for you that you do them regardless of other people's opinions.

We all go out of our way to avoid embarrassment wherever possible for obvious reasons, but if you avoid doing anything that has the potential to embarrass you, then you won't end up doing anything that feels meaningful.

Feeling foolish comes with the territory when you are on the path to achieving something important or significant. The more intimidated you are by a major life decision, the more you probably need to be doing it.

216   The state of flow

To become the best they can be, athletes continually challenge themselves by stretching their capabilities, going outside their comfort zone, and overcoming obstacles and doubts. They often describe the process of achieving total focus as being in the zone, or in a state of flow – a trance-like state in which time seems to slow down, or even stand still, and where they are totally absorbed by and unaware of anything else but the task at hand.

This flow state is accessible to you, whether you're engaged in a physical activity, a creative pursuit or even a simple day-to-day task. Flow is a source of mental energy that focuses concentration, where you lose yourself in the moment – when you find your abilities are well matched to an activity, the world around you quietens and you may find yourself achieving things you only dreamed to be possible.

217   Harsh teacher

Failure can be a highly effective teacher. It's also a harsh and unsympathetic one. The insight and value you take from things not going your way ultimately depend on which lessons you learn. If you perceive failure to be a negative judgement on your skill and ability, you'll eventually learn to dread trying anything new. You may begin to see yourself as incompetent and inadequate, and so pervasive might this dread become in your mind that you'll become unwilling to take risks.

Conversely, if you perceive failure to be nothing more than feedback, you'll recognise it as an opportunity to improve your processes. Rather than feeling incompetent due to your lack of success this time, you'll be inclined to incorporate the feedback and try again.

218   Impulse control

Short-term discomfort is an unavoidable part of developing self-discipline and mental toughness. It's important to develop an ability to tolerate discomfort. The alternative is to immediately cater to your impulses, and that's the opposite of discipline.

When you feel frustrated, annoyed or troubled in some way, embrace these feelings. Do not avoid them – acknowledge them without giving in to them. The more you learn to do this, the more you will strengthen your impulse control.

219   The story of the crow and the jug

A thirsty crow came across a jug, which was full of water. But when the crow put its beak into the jug, he could not reach the water. He kept trying but eventually gave up. At last he came up with an idea. He kept dropping pebbles into the pitcher and soon the water rose up to the top and he was able to quench his thirst.

The Lesson: Little by little does the trick. When at first you don't succeed, try, try again! Persistence is the key to solving any problem. If your first solution doesn't solve the problem, think of another solution. Look at the problem in a different way. Keep trying until you get the answer. After all, it's better than doing nothing at all.

220   Humble pie

To be humble, or practise humility, means you value other people and their opinions without indulging in self-pride. Humility is the opposite of boastfulness, arrogance and vanity, and humility has nothing to do with being meek, weak or indecisive.

Develop your humility by welcoming and seeking out new knowledge. Be curious and encourage curiosity from those around you. When you are a truly humble person, you'll display modesty, gratitude and generosity. How can you do that today?

221   Set a firm deadline

Your workload will tend to expand to fill the time you have available for its completion. More hours worked doesn't mean you necessarily get more things done. And the trouble is, you probably fill any spare time with distractions.

This is because your mind is wired to conserve energy whenever possible. If you don't have to do something, there's a good chance you won't do it. Instead, you'll allow yourself to get sucked into distractions such as apps on your phone. However, when you're up against a deadline, you suddenly develop a laser-like focus and avoid distractions at all costs. When you know you have to get something done, you'll figure out a way to do it.

To eliminate distractions, give yourself a shorter time frame to finish your work. This is like giving yourself an artificial deadline but backed up with something that holds you accountable. If it helps, ask someone to hold you accountable to make your artificial deadline more real.

However you do it, setting a firm deadline will help you avoid distractions and ramp up your productivity.

222   Ice-cold therapy

Wim Hof is the world-famous guru of cold water therapy. He has spent his life encouraging people to bathe in ice-cold water. Why? Because it increases your alertness, behavioural and cognitive performance, activates your body's natural healing powers, aids your digestion and improves your sleep, among other benefits.

Cold open-water swimming is not for the faint-hearted, but if you're up for it, it can dramatically help to alleviate symptoms of depression and anxiety. Swimming in cold, open water outdoors will burn extra calories, improve your circulation and give you an incredible natural high.

Are you mentally tough enough for this challenge?

223 Attention!

Cognitive control is the scientific term for directing your attention where you want it to be and keeping it there rather than allowing your mind to wander. People who stay calm in a crisis, who don't get rattled or agitated and recover quickly from a debacle or defeat, have good cognitive control.

Try 'brain training' games to practise holding your attention and see if you can extend the time before you get distracted by something.

224 Hint of temptation

In the same way that you can develop good habits, you can also develop bad habits. One bad habit is to give in to your impulses. The more you do this, the stronger the habit becomes and the quicker you're willing to give up when faced with adversity. Your mind has a sneaky way of convincing you to make small concessions, and when you give in to them, you don't realise you're actually training yourself to respond to the impulses you should be avoiding.

If you can resist your impulses, you'll be training your mind to tolerate short-term discomfort, and that reduces your tendency to give up at the first hint of temptation.

225 Adopt a growth mindset

Nothing about you is fixed; everything can be developed. How you are now is not how you will always be.

You can literally change your mind.

When you adopt a growth mindset you have a greater chance of reaching the outcomes you desire because you know instinctively that you have the ability to learn and develop. The hallmark of a person with a growth mindset is their relentless ability to stretch themselves and never give up, even when things aren't going well.

226 Set high standards

The standards you set yourself will have a huge effect on the quality of your life. Your standards are reflected in how you treat yourself and other people. If you're not pushing or challenging yourself, you won't be learning or growing. Settle for low standards and you'll never bring out the best in yourself.

To avoid any detrimental effect of high standards, find a healthy balance between what's important and what's not necessary. Even during tough times or when you're facing difficulties, don't lower the bar. Keep your standards high. Maintain uncompromising standards.

227 Hard work is good

Hard work is hard for everyone. Everyone needs to do things they find uncomfortable and have to work hard to tolerate. Everyone. Bill Gates does. Tony Robbins does. You do.

One of the many benefits of hard work is the confidence it builds as you start to recognise the progress you're making. Regardless of the task or mission, there isn't much of a better motivator that when you start to realise you are improving. It's even better when other people begin to notice improvements as well.

228   Never give up

It's important to pursue growth in all matters related to your commitments. Doing so exposes you to unfamiliar situations which give you an opportunity to expand your skill set beyond your knowledge base. Mentally tough people have a growth mindset. They believe their abilities are not set in stone and anything is possible. They believe and trust they can learn new abilities, often by persevering when life becomes difficult.

Mentally tough people are rarely inclined to give up – they perceive their shortcomings as areas that need improvement and setbacks as opportunities to learn from their mistakes. A growth mindset is an essential component of a positive attitude, the underlying belief that you can constantly improve yourself. Believing that you can achieve things that were impossible for you in the past is essential to becoming mentally tough. It reinforces your self-confidence, which amplifies your willingness to stay the course when you encounter adversity.

229   Always learning

Did you know that your brain is constantly rewiring itself? It's called neuroplasticity. You can train your brain to be a better problem solver by adopting more of a growth mindset. With a growth mindset you'll believe that your most basic abilities can be developed through dedication and hard work – your brains and talent are just the starting point.

With a growth mindset you'll see mistakes or setbacks as opportunities for learning. You'll focus on the process of mastering something new, to enjoy being challenged and to learn – your focus will be on the process rather than the outcome. Regardless of whether you achieve your goal, of whether the outcome is perfect, you'll notice what you've learned and how you've grown. You'll become more comfortable with making errors because you know these are opportunities for learning and improving.

You can also apply your growth mindset to your thoughts about yourself, which takes your focus off past accomplishments and towards what you've learned and how you've grown as a person.

230   Grit trumps talent

Imagine what you could accomplish if you could endure any unpleasant or difficult process or situation, without ever giving way. We usually think of endurance in terms of sport, but you can also build your endurance for life.

So, how do you discover that inner strength and how do you keep going despite feeling fatigued?

When you experience a setback, hardship or challenge, it doesn't have to result in suffering and struggle. Try simply pushing through. It may be boring. It may hurt a little and it may feel unrewarding in the moment. But hang on in there. It's so true what they say: 'Grit trumps talent.'

231   Grab on

If you're struggling, allow yourself to recognise that your struggle is valid, no matter what you're struggling with. Don't be ashamed of what makes you stressed. Then acknowledge the ways you're already resilient. Think about the toughest times you've had in your life, and how you got through those things. You probably already know a great deal about being resilient. Know your strengths and use them. Grab onto your experience and your strengths to get through whatever is in front of you.

232   Good stress

Everyone experiences stress. Stress is simply an everyday fact of life that no one can avoid. The mentally tough will handle and manage stress and pressure better than others. You can learn to do this, too.

Stress is a term borrowed from physics and engineering to describe the force of significant magnitude to distort or deform something. Stress in medical usage refers to the body's reaction to feeling threatened or under pressure. You might think of stressful events as being negative, but stress can also be a positive thing as it can help you to perform at a higher level when required. Stress can also boost your memory and your mood.

If a situation arises that puts extra demands on your time and energy, remember you can say no. You don't always have to meet the expectations of others, particularly if it will take a toll on you.

233   Goals with purpose

What's your goal? Your ability to define your goals, and the smaller, actionable steps to achieve them, will help you to develop your mental resilience. It doesn't matter how big or small your goals are, or whether they relate to your physical health, emotional wellbeing, career, finance, spirituality, or just about anything.

Goals that involve you acquiring new skills will have extra benefits because setting and working towards goals that are new to you as an individual (such as volunteering for a cause) can be especially useful in building resiliency. These goals may give you a deeper sense of purpose and connection, which you will find extremely valuable during challenging times.

Write down a goal you're working towards that extends beyond yourself and into your community.

234   Go the extra mile

List, one by one, the things you would be willing to go the extra mile for. These are the things that, regardless of failure or setbacks, you would still make an effort to do, and get up and learn from your mistakes.

Fully embrace and understand that your passion is a result of action rather than the cause of it. You won't find your passion by being complacent. It is a trial-and-error process. If you aren't willing to go out of your way to do something, then you aren't truly passionate about it.

What will you go the extra mile for?

235   Don't give up without a fight

When you're tempted to give up, ask yourself a series of probing questions to get to the heart of the matter. The answers will determine whether your urge stems from an emotional impulse or a reasoned decision.

Giving up might be a sensible option, but if an outcome is important to you, you should think hard about whether it makes sense. Why do you want to quit? Does the reward adequately compensate you for the discomfort? What is your purpose?

It's easy to forget why something is important to you – you can get lost in the process of achieving your goal and forget the reason you wanted to achieve it in the first place. Revisit your purpose and if it's still important, you'll find the resolve to press on. Otherwise you can reasonably, confidently and without regret decide to abandon your endeavour.

236   Give yourself a pat on the back

If you're lacking self-confidence, it may be because you tend to focus more on your weaknesses than your strengths, so today make a list of your strengths, talents and accomplishments. Be honest with yourself and read from this list daily to remind you of your greatness.

Write it on a piece of paper and stick it on the wall – for instance: 'I'm beautiful and talented.' It may seem like a cliché, but it works. You'll start to believe in messages you're constantly exposed to – that's why advertising is so effective. Your confidence is influenced tremendously by your daily thoughts, especially recurring thoughts.

Consistency is key to lasting change. If you want to be more confident, make a habit of reminding yourself of your unique gifts and abilities.

237   Go for risky and uncomfortable

Your comfort zone is a place where you feel comfortable and at ease, where your abilities are not being tested, where you have safe ways of existing and working, often with a familiar routine. You feel in control of your environment, with low levels of stress and anxiety. In your comfort zone you won't push yourself or uncover abilities you don't know you have. If you want to do things in a new way, you'll have to step outside your self-imposed box.

Every time you are faced with making a choice, write down one response that is safe and comfortable and one that feels risky and uncomfortable.

The risky/uncomfortable route is the one that will teach you the most and make you grow the most, so that's the one you should choose.

238   Be passionate

When you know your purpose in life, your reason for being, you'll be more deeply committed to pursuing your goals. Then it follows that you'll never have to settle for less than what you want in life. The chances are slim that your ultimate goal is to work for someone else or be someone's assistant. You probably want to create your own way.

Your goal will be fuelled by your passion. When your passion is high, your commitment is strong.

What is your reason for being?

239   Get out of your own way

Are you fully aware that you are the biggest obstacle in your own life? You may have all sorts of reasons why you don't get things done, and many of the reasons may be outside your control. But instead of focusing on the things you can't control, focus on your biggest barrier, the one you have most control over: you!

Get out of your own way by reminding yourself why you are doing something. Humans hate to do things for no reason... so what's your reason? Whatever the task you face, it must contribute to some larger purpose. Becoming a mentally strong person takes practice and mindfulness. It requires a deep understanding of your own mission/purpose/reason. And sometimes it simply means learning to get out of your own way and let things happen.

What is your purpose?

240   Ditch the familiar

We tend to stick to things that are familiar to us – we visit the same restaurants, we participate in the same activities with our friends. We even stay in unhealthy relationships because we know what to expect.

Uncertainty is uncomfortable, and most of us try to avoid that feeling wherever possible. No one relishes feeling uncomfortable or exposed to uncertainty. Most of us favour predictability because it poses less risk. The problem is, staying inside your comfort zone insulates you from experiences that may hold valuable lessons. If you never try new things or take calculated risks, you rob yourself of the opportunity to grow.

If you continually cocoon yourself from uncertainty, you will never give yourself a chance to truly develop your mental toughness. Your newly found tougher mindset is like a muscle that needs regular exercise, so you'll need to practise getting out of your comfort zone on a daily basis.

CHAPTER 9

FIND WHAT YOU'RE MADE OF

241 The story of the bell and the cat

A family of mice had been living in fear because of a cat. One day they came together to discuss possible ideas to defeat the cat. After much discussion, one young mouse got up to propose an idea. He suggested that they put a bell around the cat's neck, so they could hear it when it approached. All the other mice thought it was a great plan, apart from one wise old mouse. The old mouse liked the plan in theory, but asked: 'Who will put the bell on the cat?'

The Lesson: It's easy to propose impossible remedies. Having lots of ideas is good for problem solving, but having ideas that work is even better. It's never a good idea to shout about an idea until you know it's going to work. Remember, people want straightforward solutions, not more problems.

242 Take risks

Successful people are risk takers. To achieve the success you desire, you must be willing to expand a little and take some risks. Quite often, taking risks can create delightful experiences and feelings. Stay risk averse and you'll create a stifling and rigid attitude towards change, so much so that you could experience great stress when change does occur. Change is inevitable. The only constant is change. Change will happen no matter how carefully you try to avoid it, so get comfortable being uncomfortable.

243 Keep your finger on the pulse

You can use technology to help build your mental toughness – there are some very cool gadgets to help you do this. A pulse oximeter, worn on your wrist like a watch, is a non-invasive and painless test that measures your oxygen saturation level or the oxygen levels in your blood, checking how well your heart is pumping oxygen through your body. It can rapidly detect even small changes in how efficiently oxygen is being carried to the extremities farthest from your heart, including your legs and your arms.

A better understanding of your physical state, and especially your oxygen levels, will alert you to improving things so that you're able to concentrate and focus better and for longer.

244   Get back to happy

If you always do what you've always done, you'll always get what you've always got.

If you always avoid difficult conversations, you'll always work with people that aren't up to scratch.

If you always blame others, you'll never take ownership and you'll never be the best you can be.

Everything that happens is a cyclical process that will continue until you make an intervention – a change that puts you on a new course. If you feel like you're missing something, then make a change – somewhere, anywhere. If what you're putting out there isn't working, or isn't manifesting the results you want, you are the only one that can get you back on the way to happy.

245   Face your fear

The fear you have may be at the root of a lack of self-confidence. When you're scared of the outcome of something, you aren't likely to go into it feeling assured. Until you face your fear head on, it controls you and makes the voice of self-doubt louder.

Think about a fear you faced and recall how you felt afterwards. Perhaps you felt liberated and proud. You might have even wanted to do the thing you were afraid of again.

Make a commitment to do something that scares you every day, once a week or once a month and watch your confidence quickly grow.

246 Form new habits

Commitment is not only a promise that you make with yourself to achieve something, it's also the dedication to give your time and energy to a specific task, enthusiastically.

Form a new set of good habits by repeating them each day for at least three weeks. If you stay fully, 100 per cent committed to practising new good habits, then the chances of success greatly increase. With an optimistic mindset, you will be able to face any obstacle, challenge or setback. Challenges will come and go, but when you stay determined and optimistic, you'll manage everything with a positive attitude.

Keep your focus on your main goal while making your new good habits a part of your life.

247 Forgive yourself

Forgiveness can be defined as a deliberate decision to let go of your feelings of anger, resentment and desire for retribution towards someone whom you believe has wronged you. However, while you may be quite generous in your ability to forgive others, you might be much harder on yourself.

Everyone makes mistakes, but learning how to learn from these errors, let go, move on and forgive yourself is important for your sense of wellbeing. If you're not used to self-forgiveness, you might find it isn't easy at first. But if you're going to pick yourself up and move on, it's going to be a necessity. Beating yourself up is not productive and can be very damaging.

If it doesn't come naturally to forgive yourself, then keep practising, and remember: everything takes time.

248   Focus on now

If you're anything like me, there will be some decisions you've made in your life that you regret or would change. Past mistakes can haunt us and leave us struggling to move forward. Perhaps you've had to accept some devastating life circumstances.

In any case, you can start to accept the things you cannot change by focusing on what you can do now. You may not be able to do anything about what has passed, but you can do something to make your life better today. Your current mood will be affected by your diet, the amount of sleep you get and the level at which you take regular exercise.

Forgive yourself for your past mistakes with the same level of compassion you would show a friend. Find the lesson from what you experienced and accept that what has happened, has happened.

249   Flip it

Your brain has a natural tendency to give weight to and remember negative experiences more than positive ones. They stand out more.

This 'negative bias' means it's easy for the brain to create an anxious, fearful state out of any situation where you're less likely to find a solution. By focusing on negative things you reshape your perception into seeing negative things. Before you know it, you're in a very unhelpful loop.

The good news is that the flip side is also true – focus on the positive and you'll see positive outcomes. Try to maintain a hopeful, optimistic outlook and expect a positive outcome instead of a negative one. Visualisation can be a helpful technique to see a brighter picture.

250   Fear of failure

One of the fastest ways to healing is to look at what you have, not what you don't have. Having daily gratitude is powerful. This goes with failures and setbacks as well. Find a way to be grateful for what has happened and what you've been able to learn from it.

Believe it or not, the most satisfying victory is usually the one that was the most difficult. So be grateful for the journey, no matter how treacherous. If you stick with it, hang on, there's beauty to be had.

251   First things first

First things first. Second things never.

If everything is important, then nothing is. Focus your time and attention on what moves your dial, floats your boat or feels purposeful.

With a clear purpose you'll feel more energised and motivated.

252   Finding fortitude

There's no doubt you have, and will, face times when nothing goes according to plan and you just feel like giving up. These times are the most crucial points in your life and the decisions you make will affect you for the rest of your life.

Fortitude (your ability to focus on and execute solutions when faced with uncertainty or adversity) is what ultimately makes you as a person.

It is what all great people are capable of, no matter how bad the situation. If you crack under pressure, or lose patience with the process you're being challenged with, it can easily drive you to quit prematurely. Having the mental fortitude necessary to succeed requires patience, creativity, exploration and execution.

When you can develop the mental fortitude necessary to stay strong in the face of adversity, you will reduce the intensity of the fear you face.

253   Loving support

Many factors will contribute to your resilience, but the primary factor is going to be about having supportive relationships within and outside of your family. Relationships that are caring, loving and offer encouragement and reassurance will help you to cultivate your resilience.

Other factors associated with resilience are things you can develop within yourself, such as your capacity to make realistic plans and actionable steps to carry them out, a positive self-view and confidence in your strengths and abilities, your communication and problem-solving skills, your capacity to manage and regulate strong feelings and impulses.

254   Find your block

When you perceive that you have the power to determine your fate, you're likely to be happier, healthier and more productive. Even the most challenging events are more bearable when you feel you have some say in the outcome.

If you feel helpless and unable to change a situation, you're more likely to get stressed and anxious because powerlessness is inherently threatening. Having a greater sense of control of your life will help you to make important decisions and stay on track when times get tough.

Reframe your thoughts, put your challenge into perspective and identify one thing, however small, that could be blocking you from having a greater sense of control of your destiny.

255   Find the silver linings

Your ability to find the silver linings in stressful or difficult situations will help you to generate positive emotions, even when there is nothing obviously positive in your situation.

Finding silver linings can help you to counteract negative emotions, decrease stress and quicken your recovery from stressful events.

Try it first by recalling a project that didn't work out the way you'd hoped. Now, reflect on that situation again and this time find the silver linings. How could the situation have been worse? What were opportunities that resulted from that situation? What were the positives?

Think of as many silver linings as you can. Be as creative as possible and think of anything, however small, that would have made you feel better about that experience.

256   Stay in the moment

If you experience low moods or bouts of mild depression, they can get worse if you are focusing on a particular issue in the past or future. Try, as much as possible, to stay in the present moment. Focusing on issues you can't change or control can also make you feel anxious or stressed. Staying in the present and focusing on what you can change and influence today is the key.

257   Find the right question

You have a problem or an issue and you don't know the right answer. You have all sorts of scenarios and options whizzing around your head and you have no idea what the best way forward is.

STOP.

Pause and consider: What is the real question I need to ask myself here? What is lying behind all of this? Trying to find the right question is far more useful than finding lots of answers.

Asking yourself this big fundamental question will narrow down your options and get to the real issue, making your decision-making process far easier.

So, what is the big question you need to ask yourself?

258   Find the benefits of past challenges

Part of what makes challenges, well, challenging is that we become short-sighted and focus only on the bad, without seeing the good. So how do you find the benefits of failure?

People may tell you that you should take action and reflect on your failures right after you experience them. But negative emotions can cloud your thinking. If you're still feeling upset about a failure, it may be harder to see the benefits or come up with effective solutions.

Start finding the benefits of challenges by looking at past ones – challenges that you're no longer upset about. Keep practising this so that you can strengthen your ability to find the benefits next time. A good exercise is to write out a list of things you learned from a past failure. For example, if you missed an important deadline, maybe you learned that you need to prioritise better, delegate more or tone down your perfectionism. Try to really search for as many benefits as you can think of.

259   Failure is life's best teacher

I have never liked using the word 'failure'. I think it's because it sounds so negative, but in fact when things don't go your way, you have a wonderful opportunity to learn, improve and go again. I welcome 'failure' because it offers new perspectives: it can help you to refocus and find new solutions and strategies. If things had all gone your way, what would you have learned? If you win at everything you try, you don't learn too much! Failure is the best teacher in life. What has recently not gone your way? What can you see from this situation as an opportunity to grow and improve instead of a reason to give up? Be willing to keep trying until you get it right.

260   Find the light in the shade

Practise finding the benefits of every seemingly negative situation you face. First, think about something that happened recently that wasn't a great experience. Try not to choose an experience that was really bad – it's important to consider something that wasn't too awful when you're first learning how to use this technique. You can work up to harder experiences as you become more skilled.

Now brainstorm potential ways you could have dealt with the situation to get some learning from it. You're likely to have had more options than you might think. Spend time contemplating how you could have responded to that tough situation. Even if you couldn't entirely fix it, you can always develop plans to cope with tricky situations. Next time you face a setback, brainstorm five positive ways you can address it, to extract some learning from it.

261   Find out what you're made of

Once you find the courage to move out of your comfort zone, you immediately prove to yourself that you're capable of achieving more than you thought was possible. And that will change the way you see yourself. Moving forward, you'll have more confidence in yourself whenever you step out of your comfort zone, and that increased confidence will make it more likely that you continue to step outside your comfort zone. And each time you do, you'll prove to yourself again and again what you're really capable of.

262   Make quality a habit

Greek philosophers 2,500 years ago, such as Socrates, Plato and Aristotle, taught valuable lessons on how to live that are still powerful today. Look up some of their quotations to keep you motivated and remember to make quality a habit rather than an occasional effort.

If you want to improve your performance or beat the competition, then your emphasis on quality has to be consistent.

263   Focus blocks

Focus is intense interest in action. It's like shining a spotlight. When you're focused, you notice only what you pay attention to. You're truly focused when your thoughts and actions coincide. You will lose concentration and become distracted when your focus moves to irrelevant matters or factors.

Focus gives you the single-mindedness to get rid of all distractions irrelevant to the task at hand. Improve your powers of focus by becoming aware of the blocks to your concentration.

264   Fill in the blank

The life you want is on the other side of the sh*t you don't want to do.

You're bound to avoid the things that make you uncomfortable, but there is no growth in the status quo. The things that are preventing you from achieving are not external, they are internal. It's easy to think that other forces are blocking your path. But that's not true – you are your biggest obstacle.

Whatever it is that you are avoiding or putting off is the thing that will make the biggest difference to your progress. Fill in the blank: I would be able to achieve my goal if only I was able to _____.

265   Feeling confident

Your level of confidence will be directly related to the healthy self-image you have of yourself. The way you see yourself creates a belief in you that says you have the abilities or skills necessary to deliver a performance outcome. Confidence is the feeling that you're able to do what you need to do, when you need to do it. Your self-image and confidence have developed over the years and have been shaped by your learned, cumulative experiences. Be aware of the relationship that will always exist between your level of confidence and the performance you deliver.

266   Don't talk so much

'Know how to listen and you will profit even from those who talk badly,' wrote the first-century CE Greek philosopher and biographer Plutarch.

You probably talk way too much and listen too little. When you focus on listening to those around you, you can better understand people's ideas, problems and desires.

Practise 'active listening' by asking open-ended questions that get to the root of people's problems or issues. The more questions you ask (and the more you listen), the more information you will receive, which will provide you with what you need to deliver.

Often the best advice comes from those who have experienced life before us and have discovered how to successfully navigate through troubled waters to find the right path. The struggles we have today are not new; it is simply the human condition. What we can learn from the ancient Greeks is just as relevant now as it was two millennia or more ago.

267   Fear becomes focus

When you commit 100 per cent to your goal, it becomes your sole focus. This means you can bring all your emotional energy to bear to accomplish your goal because you have one defined course of action. Commit anything less than 100 per cent and fear can sneak in and suck away your energy. Even with a 99 per cent commitment your energy will flow to alternative options, scenarios and possible failures. Don't get distracted by options. Stay laser-focused and 100 per cent committed.

268   Fall in love with the here and now

Whenever you face a challenge, there is an opportunity for you to demonstrate and develop your will and determination. Your mental toughness refers to your ability to stay strong in the face of adversity, to maintain your focus and determination despite the difficulties you encounter. A mentally tough person sees challenge and adversity as an opportunity and not a threat, and has the confidence and positive approach to take what comes in their stride.

A great way to start seeing the opportunity in every challenge is to stay focused on the 'here and now'. You'll start to see that challenges take place in your present moment. When you can put the challenge in the context of 'here and now', you'll be more able to address the challenge, learn from it and move on.

269   Fake it till you make it

Is it true that you can 'fake it till you make it'? Actually, it is.

If you want to feel more confident, then you can, as long as you correctly identify the things that are holding you back. When you find yourself feeling nervous and unsure, stop for a moment, close your eyes and think of a time when you felt confident and self-assured. Use all of your senses to bring you back to that moment.

In doing this, you'll be more able to cultivate that feeling in the present moment. Choose a body posture that makes you look and feel confident. Dress in a way that makes you feel good. If you look good to you, you'll feel good, and feeling good often leads to higher self-confidence.

270   Fail over and over

Michael Jordan, the basketball superstar, has spoken about all the missed shots, lost games and failures during his life. Yet those were the very things that spurred him on to succeed.

Your perception of failure dictates the lessons you learn from it. Learn to see through the appropriate lens that failure can have a remarkably positive effect on the development of your mental toughness.

CHAPTER 10

EMBRACE THE CHALLENGE

271   The story of the ant and the grasshopper

A grasshopper spent his summer singing and dancing while a team of ants worked hard all summer collecting food for the winter. The grasshopper didn't understand why the ants worked so hard. When winter came, the grasshopper found himself dying of hunger and saw the ants serving up food to survive. He finally understood why the ants had worked so hard.

The Lesson: There's a time for work and a time for play. Just because you don't think something is important right now doesn't mean you should ignore it or put it off. It's OK to have fun, but make sure your work is done beforehand and always be prepared for what's ahead.

272   Expand your horizons

The good thing about your comfort zone is that it's flexible and malleable. With each action you take outside of your comfort zone, it expands. And once you master that new skill or action, it eventually becomes part of your comfort zone. This is great news because it means that you can constantly increase and improve the behaviours that you're comfortable with. And the more tools and skills you have at your disposal, the easier it will be to achieve your goals and the mentally tougher you will become.

273   Every mistake is a lesson

Henry Ford wisely said, 'The only real mistake is the one from which we learn nothing.' No one likes making mistakes – they can be embarrassing and humiliating – but thankfully there is upside to making mistakes. Your mistakes will help your growth mindset – your belief that your intelligence is something that can be developed. If you never make a mistake, it means you are never doing anything or moving forward. Embrace the mistake and search for the lesson.

274 Exercise that muscle

Most of us enjoy familiarity. We tend to stick to things we know: same restaurants, same friends, same meals. Lots of people even stay in unhealthy relationships because they know what to expect. For many, uncertainty is uncomfortable and that's a feeling we like to avoid. Trouble is, if you stay inside your comfort zone, you'll miss out on experiences that may hold valuable lessons for you. If you never try new things, never take calculated risks, you will be robbing yourself of the opportunity to grow. Don't cocoon yourself from uncertainty. Getting out of your comfort zone regularly will develop your mental toughness – and mental toughness is like a muscle: it needs regular exercise.

275 Empathy

Don't confuse 'empathy' with being nice. It's much more than that. Being empathetic means you can put yourself into another person's shoes and acknowledge their emotions in light of their circumstances. You're able to understand their thoughts and feelings in that moment.

When you're able to gain an insight into myriad adverse situations experienced by others, you're able to achieve more clarity when you experience similar situations yourself. Then you're building your mental toughness.

Empathy allows you to connect to others, at a deeper level, and what could be better than that?

276   Start now, get perfect later

Enough of the talking, start taking action. Just start. Start by doing one press-up, reading one page, making one sale, attending one seminar, writing one paragraph. Start today, repeat tomorrow.

It's really important that whatever you're dreaming of is not left undone. Your project or goal will not happen if you procrastinate. Don't give up or put it off. Your words are blown away with the wind. Action is necessary for your plan to move forward.

What action will you take today?

277   Emotional mastery

No one achieves emotional mastery overnight. The good news is, if you take action every day, you'll eventually be able to manage your emotions whenever you experience difficult situations.

Make a list of the negative emotions you typically experience when things go wrong. Maybe it's anger, maybe it's despair, guilt or apathy. Whatever the case, write it down. Then carefully think about each emotion you've identified in your list and write a short note next to it that describes how it affects your behaviour. For example, feeling angry might cause you to lash out at others.

Now write a short note next to each negative emotion that describes how you *intend* to respond to it in the future. For example, if you feel angry, you might commit to taking five deep breaths.

278   Decisions, decisions

Do you ever find yourself unable to take decisive action because you're paralysed by the consequences of making the wrong decision?

Or maybe you're worried about what other people will think of your decision? Or it simply doesn't feel right?

Take a moment to consider the consequences of continuing to procrastinate or delay a decision and gather more information, versus the cost of making a poor decision or choice. Quite often, any action is better than no action. So make a choice, because you will always have the opportunity to learn from the decision you make.

Instead of shying away from problems and decisions, wishing they would just disappear, try to take decisive action whenever possible. Decisive people are often the most successful.

279   Do it for free

What job would you do for free if you didn't need the salary? Do you work to live or do you live to work? If you are doing something that you are passionate about, it won't feel like work. There will never be a Sunday night when you are dreading the imminent Monday morning.

What part of your work comes easy to you because you are happy while you're doing it? Aligning your professional life with your purpose is a critical part of living out your purpose on planet Earth.

280   Embrace pressure to make the decision

What happens when you're required to make good decisions under pressure? You're going to need to maintain some emotional stability. It's important that you also maintain your capacity to stay objective and deliver decisions regardless of what you're feeling. Knowledge is power.

The first step to making decisions under pressure is to really know and understand the situation. The better you understand the situation and all that it entails, the more likely you are to make a good decision.

When you're faced with a tough decision under pressure, gather as much information as you can, the big-picture stuff alongside the smaller detail.

281   Embrace optimism

Maintaining a positive attitude and suppressing negative self-talk involves you developing the ability to highlight your strengths and celebrate the successes, as well as recognising your weaknesses and blunders as opportunities to learn and grow.

Sadly, many of us learn to be pessimistic about ourselves, thanks to the setbacks and disappointments we have experienced in our lives. This attitude not only hampers your confidence, it also prevents you from growing.

The good news is that you can recondition your mind to embrace optimism and positive thinking. You can retrain yourself to instinctively recognise your ability to overcome adversity. You can become mentally tough!

282   Do the opposite

Listen to advice carefully, then do the exact opposite.

We all have some form of inner rebel that likes to question or do the opposite of what we're told. This is called 'psychological reactance'. It's your brain's reaction to when you feel a threat to your freedom or think your choices are being limited.

When someone discourages you from doing something, you feel that your freedom is being threatened, which can motivate you to regain choice and control by doing exactly the opposite.

When someone tells you not to think about something, your mind has a sneaky way of returning to that very thought... don't think of a pink elephant!

When your behaviour is forbidden or discouraged by others, it's hard not to become intrigued and to want to do it more.

It's good to be a rebel, so embrace your psychological reactance today.

283   Embrace negative thoughts

Negative emotions are natural and they can be useful in focusing your attention and spurring you to improve yourself. The problem is, emotions like anxiety, anger and fear can overwhelm you and paralyse you into inaction. A little goes a long way, but too much can quickly overload you.

Nevertheless, don't suppress your negative emotions – instead, learn to manage them. Ask yourself whether your feelings align with logic and reason – when they're in sync, you'll find it much easier to take purposeful action and make good decisions when things go wrong.

It's not always easy to control negative emotions, but the more consistent you are in using these techniques, the easier it becomes.

284   Don't allow insecurity to breed inaction

It's difficult to stay mentally tough through setbacks when you lack confidence in your abilities and skills. But ability and skill deficits are rarely the main factor in determining whether you succeed or fail. The deciding factor is usually insecurity.

Insecurity breeds inaction, which is a much larger threat to your success. There's nothing wrong with feeling self-doubt. It's natural. It's your brain's way of protecting you for the hard work ahead. The trouble starts if you allow self-doubt to get a foothold in your mind to the point that it paralyses you and all of your energy becomes focused on your perceived deficits.

Be very careful not to allow your insecurities to incapacitate you.

285   Embrace change

Flexibility is an essential part of building your resilience and resilient people have an uncanny ability to flex and shift when their circumstances change. Instead of being paralysed by things being unexpectedly different, you can learn to quickly adapt and respond by changing the one thing you have control over: yourself.

By learning how to be more adaptable and flexible, you'll be better equipped to respond when you are faced with a setback or life crisis. While some people may be crushed by abrupt changes, highly resilient individuals will adapt and thrive.

286   Please yourself

Do you have the right attitude towards the setbacks you face? Complications, unintended consequences, side effects and complete failures are all aspects of the landscape you will face. It's all just part of a normal life. So when you can mitigate the damage and learn lessons from every challenge, you'll be more ready for what lies ahead in the future.

Don't worry about pleasing others because that's a valueless 'hit or miss' proposition. Instead, make a concentrated effort to do what is right and to know what you stand for. But what does matter to you? Write a list of your top 10 priorities and values and stand by them every day of your life.

287   Doubt your doubt

Doubt is the enemy of confidence. Doubt keeps you feeling uncertain and can make you a bit cynical. If you start doubting yourself, counteract it by doubting your doubt. Question the truth of what it is telling you. Your doubt might be saying, 'I'm really not good at this.' Question your limiting beliefs whenever they arise. You'll likely realise there aren't many facts to back up the doubtful assertion.

288   Tough talk

When you're stressed, your body releases cortisol. Cortisol stimulates the release of adrenaline and noradrenaline, causing the 'fight or flight' physical response in you. With too much cortisol coursing through your body, you're at risk of a host of mental and physical health problems, from anxiety to weight gain to heart disease.

Your cortisol levels in your blood, urine or saliva can be tested at home using a home testing kit that is sent to a lab for results. Monitoring your cortisol levels is a great way to know how well you're developing your mental toughness.

289   Emotional management

Life will become more enjoyable when you can learn to manage your emotions in a way that positively impacts your life and performance, every day. Your emotional responses to situations are due to every one of your experiences up until today – emotions like frustration, happiness, anger, success, failure and joy.

To lift your mood, start by identifying what particular thought has triggered your low mood. Reframing that thought to a positive one will change your mood, and that in turn will change your behaviour and move you towards the life you desire.

290   Put your energy into the things you can control

Don't dwell on something you can't change. When you find yourself worrying, take a minute to examine the things you have control over. You can't prevent a storm from coming, but you can prepare for it. You can't control how someone else behaves, but you can control how you react.

Recognise that, sometimes, all you can control is your effort and your attitude. When you put your energy into the things you can control, you'll be much more effective. You can influence people and circumstances, but you can't force things to go your way. To have the most influence, focus on changing your behaviour. Don't try to fix people who don't want to be fixed. Move on and make way for something better to come along.

291   Take your time

Time is not always a healer because trauma can be very hard to recover from. Your emotional responses to being wounded are often complex, and, like peeling an onion, they may have to be addressed one layer at a time.

To recover from trauma, your brain has to learn to stay at least partially in the present experience, something that often requires therapeutic assistance. The passage of time may take the edge off acute pain, but it doesn't always heal all the pain you feel.

Embracing the passage of time can help start the healing process though. Take some time today to think about the events in your life that have led you to feeling wounded. Identify the source of the pain as this will help you begin the journey of healing and let you feel more optimistic about the new possibilities that lie ahead.

292   Do the hardest one first

I am guessing you keep a list of things you need to get done. Have you ever noticed that you scan through your to-do list and focus on the easiest items first?

From now on, scan the list daily and find the toughest, most challenging thing on the list – the thing you tend to put off to another day – and do it immediately. Do it first! Attending to this is likely to have a more profound outcome than anything else on the list.

You'll be surprised how pleased with yourself you feel for doing it. You will have an outcome and you'll be free to work through the rest of your list knowing that you've already done the hard part.

293   Be competent

You could say being competent is more useful than being confident because it's all about being brilliant, not just feeling brilliant. When you are competent you can see your success objectively, which is likely to make you feel pretty good about yourself.

Identify ways you can get better at what you do because that is you taking action. It is taking action that will propel you forward. Forget feeling like you're good at something and focus instead on finding out how good you really are. Then you can identify and build on your strengths and know your areas for development, and decide what you want to do about them.

294   Do it over, and over, and over

Do anything many times over and you'll get better at it, whatever it is. Repeated, deliberate practice of anything improves performance, experience and confidence. This applies to daily habits, too. The more often you repeat the same behaviours or habits, the more ingrained and easier they become.

If you're trying to develop a new set of good habits, don't try to fix a lot of things in a short space of time. It's better to make small, effective adjustments on a couple of things, so that your mind can adjust to these gradual, positive changes.

Building your mental toughness is no different... developing daily habits builds mental 'muscle'.

295   The power of vulnerability

Be more vulnerable. It requires strength to be honest. To wear your heart on your sleeve and admit you might be struggling. It's OK to say you don't know the answers or admit you lack a certain skill. Admit your shortcomings, but do it with a sense of confidence. Confidence is about exerting control of the situation; vulnerability is about reacting to the situation.

It's not a weakness to be honest and to show vulnerability. You don't need to be strong all the time, and being vulnerable will help you to make new friends and see things from new perspectives. Dip your toe into the world of vulnerability.

296   Do it anyway

Successful people have a much higher tolerance for always being 'on', for pushing past discomfort and doing what needs to be done. The ones that get ahead tolerate an immense amount of discomfort, so much that it no longer becomes uncomfortable. What is it that you cannot tolerate? Think about something that's so uncomfortable you've been putting it off. And do it anyway. The only way out is through.

297 Develop your self-belief

Having a strong, deep and genuine belief in your own ability – your self-confidence – is what you'll need to take the decisive actions you need to take, to get what you want. Believing in yourself, and in your ability, is critical to creating the life you desire.

The good news is that you are in the driving seat here. You can start by shifting your perspective on failure to simply seeing any failure as an opportunity to learn how to do things better or differently next time. Your failures are not obstacles – they are gifts and opportunities to learn. The more you learn and experience, the more your confidence grows.

298 Do something you think you can't do

When there's something you really don't want to do, like tackle a boring report, tell yourself you only have to do it for 10 minutes. When the 10-minute mark rolls around, allow yourself to stop, if you want to. Chances are, though, you'll keep going (starting is usually the hardest part).

Starting something you don't want to do trains your brain to know that you don't have to respond to how you feel. Just because you don't feel like doing it doesn't mean you can't do it. You're stronger than you think, and you can take action even when you're not motivated to.

This applies to taking on more significant challenges, too. When your brain tries to talk you out of doing something, practise responding with 'Challenge accepted!;

Your brain underestimates you, but every time you do something that you thought you couldn't do, you challenge it to start seeing you as more capable and competent than it gives you credit for.

299   Deciding what's best

Imagine how wonderful it would be if you had a special tool to help you decide what is right for you. I have good news for you... you already do! It's called your inner compass. It's an amazingly accurate and reliable resource that is working all the time to guide you and give you information about what is best for you.

Your inner compass also has the ability to help you figure out whether your thoughts and actions are aligned with your values and standards. When things are aligned, you'll have a sense of comfort, ease and flow in your life. When you feel discomfort and unease, stop and check your inner compass.

When your sense of direction is deeply internalised, you never have to worry about becoming lost. Stay true to your course.

300   How do you want people to remember you?

Imagine what you would do if you only had a year left to live. Death forces you to focus on the truly important things. Thinking about what you'd do can lead you to realise what your 'life's purpose' is and allow you to let go of things that are trivial or distracting. Death may be the only thing that can give you a clear perspective on the value of your life.

How do you want people to remember you? If you don't feel that you have a sense of direction or purpose, it is because you haven't figured out what's important to you or what your values are. And if you aren't living in line with your own values, whose values or priorities are you living for?

Discovering your 'why' in life means that you have found a way to spend your limited amount of time here on Earth well.

CHAPTER 11

MENTAL MUSCLE

301   The story of the frog in hot water

A frog fell into a pan of hot water. The water was still on a gas stove. The frog didn't try to jump out of the pan but instead just stayed in it. As the temperature of the water started to rise, the frog managed to adjust his body temperature accordingly. But as the water started to reach boiling point, the frog found he could no longer manage his own temperature and couldn't bear the heat, so he tried to jump out of the pan. But he couldn't get out and died.

The Lesson: The moral of this tale is that the frog couldn't make it out due to his inability to decide when he had to jump. You'll need to adjust to situations before it's too late. Think ahead and allow yourself to walk out, before you need to jump.

302   Practise gratitude

Maintaining a positive outlook and mindset is critical to being able to face adversity with courage.

Every morning, reflect on things that have gone right for you.

Every afternoon, think about everything for which you are thankful.

Each evening before you go to bed, contemplate the small victories you enjoyed throughout the day.

Practise gratitude daily and you'll be developing mental toughness.

303   Create your future self

If you don't have a future you're actively striving for, then you can't actively convert your experience into learning. And without learning, you're likely to repeat your same old experiences over and over. Life will become routine and dull, and you will become predictable and dull.

The only way to have a powerful 'present' is by advancing courageously towards a specific 'future'. When you're committed to a bigger future, your present becomes far less predictable. Rather than living within the confines of your narrow comfort zone, you can begin to embrace uncertainty. You can start to step outside of your known world and begin approaching the world of your future self.

When this becomes your situation, your past stops being the thing predicting your personality and behaviour. Instead, your future self becomes the thing predicting your personality and behaviour.

304   Build daily habits

Motivation is fickle. Willpower comes and goes. Mental toughness isn't about getting an incredible dose of inspiration or courage; it's about building the daily habits that allow you to stick to a schedule and overcome challenges and distractions over and over and over again.

Mentally tough people don't have to be more courageous, more talented, more intelligent – just more consistent. Mentally tough people develop systems that help them focus on the important stuff regardless of how many obstacles life puts in front of them. It's their habits that form the foundation of their mental beliefs and ultimately set them apart.

Build new habits by focusing on small behaviours, not life-changing transformations. Develop a routine that gets you going regardless of how motivated you feel. Stick to your schedule and forget about the results. When you slip up, get back on track as quickly as possible.

305   Create control

One essential part of building your mental toughness is creating a feeling of mental and physical strength. When you feel mentally and physically strong, you feel more in control. Taking regular exercise strengthens your heart and improves your circulation. This increases blood flow and raises oxygen levels in your body.

All good so far. It gets better. The increased oxygen helps you to think more clearly, lowers your blood pressure, improves sleep and helps with weight loss. The endorphins you'll release are natural painkillers and will lift your mood and reduce anxiety. What are you waiting for? Find time every day for some form of physical exercise.

306   Create a challenge mindset

Do you try to avoid failure at all costs? Do you worry that people will think poorly of you if you fail? Do you feel ashamed when you fail to reach important goals?

If you think failure is a threat, your body will prepare for a fight and you'll feel like you're in a battle. But if you adopt a mindset that doing something hard, something you could fail at, is a challenge, then you're more likely to think you are capable of handling it. When you view things that you could possibly fail at as challenges, you'll actually be more capable, and less likely to fail at them.

To build your 'challenge mindset', reflect on past challenges that you've overcome. Remind yourself that you've been successful at things in the past, even small things. Next, visualise success. By imagining yourself doing well, you'll shift your mindset to do well. Keep in mind that even if you're able to shift your brain to stop seeing something as a threat, you may feel nervousness or anxiety, but you'll also experience positive physiological changes that can help you make better use of these negative emotions.

307   Control the exposure

Controlled exposure is the gradual exposure to anxiety-provoking situations. It is used to help people overcome their fears. This experience can also foster resilience, and especially so when it involves acquiring new skills and setting goals. Public speaking, for example, is a useful life skill but also something that evokes fear in many people. If you're afraid of public speaking, you can set goals involving controlled exposure, in order to develop this skill.

You can start with a small audience of one or two people and progressively increase the audience size over time. Successful controlled exposure can increase your self-esteem and a sense of autonomy and mastery, all of which can be utilised in times of adversity.

308   Contagious emotions

It's impossible not to be affected by those around you because you inevitably 'catch' their emotions. Just like a virus, emotions are contagious! Walk into a room of stressed-out people and you'll start to feel stressed yourself.

Make a conscious effort to mix with people who have high energy and you'll find yourself immediately feeling more energetic. Surround yourself by people who are encouraging and supportive and who inspire you. You are only as great as the company you keep!

309   Confident? It's your choice

What is confidence anyway? You might think of it as something that the lucky few are born with and the rest are left wishing for. Not true. Confidence is not a fixed attribute, it's the outcome of the thoughts you think and the actions you take. No more, no less. It is not based on your actual ability to succeed at a task but your belief in your ability to succeed.

The good news is that you can literally rewire your brain in ways that affect your thoughts and behaviour. This means that, no matter how timid or doubt-laden you've been up to now, building self-confidence is largely a choice you make. With consistent effort, and the courage to take a risk, you can gradually expand your confidence and your capacity to build more of it.

Don't become overly reliant on external affirmation to prop up your self-worth but take ownership of the actions needed to sustain it.

310 Overcommit deeply

Being committed means you will make a solid, well-thought-out plan that shows the best path to achieving your goals. True commitment means sticking to a plan, only deviating to avoid obstacles. That's difficult enough, but if you want to become great at what you do, you may have to *over*commit.

Instead of writing two pages, write three. Instead of speaking to four people, speak to six. Instead of running five miles, run six. When you embrace the level of commitment required, you are clear about your purpose and your passion is deep, you will reach your goal.

311 Do it on purpose

Gaining a deeper sense of purpose in your life helps you to develop resilience. It makes you better at finding meaning in setbacks you may experience, compared with those who wander through life aimlessly. When you know your purpose, you have a feeling of mastery that helps you let go of anything that goes wrong in your life that is irrelevant to your core values. This means that you can learn from life's hardships and bounce back quickly from adversity.

312   Assign value

When you commit to something, you assign value to it. The outcome you seek becomes worthy of the time and effort required to pursue it. Your actions and decisions become focused on making it a reality. Your commitment not only encourages you to exert effort towards achieving your desired outcome, it also coaxes you to persist when things fail or don't go your way.

Committing to a task, project or specific outcome gives you the resilience to stay positive and resolute when you face obstacles. Your commitment helps you to enjoy it, when giving up would be easier. It allows you to persist working towards your goals rather than surrendering them for short-term gratification.

313   Choose or change

Whatever you are not changing, you are choosing. Read that again. The mentally tough develop influence by teaching and showing people how to think and challenging them to grow. Teach people how to think and you change their lives. The mentally tough say things like 'Think of it this way' or 'What if we approached it this way?' or 'What do you think about this?' Over time, they encourage the people around them how to think because when you impact someone else's thoughts in a positive way, you have influence. But that's not all they do.

Think of an influential person in your life – maybe a parent, teacher or colleague – someone who has had an impact on you. They taught you how to think about yourself, or about others, or about the world, and they also challenged you to grow. Why was this person so influential? They inspired you, but how? They pushed you, but how did they push you? They always told you to be your best. The mentally tough challenge the people they care about to grow.

314   Chill

If you're feeling under a lot of stress, you may find that it's more difficult to manage your emotions. Even people who are generally good at controlling their emotions may well find it harder in times of high tension and stress. Reducing stress, or finding more helpful ways to deal with it, can help your emotions become more manageable.

Mindfulness practices like meditation can help with stress, too. They won't get rid of it, but they can make it easier to live with. Make sure you're getting enough sleep, make time to talk (and laugh) with friends, take plenty of exercise (especially in nature) or make time for your favourite relaxation activity or hobby.

315   An exercise in gratitude

Write down three things you are thankful for and why. It might be your job, your relationship, your ability to feed your family.

When you express gratitude and receive the same, your brain releases dopamine and serotonin, the 'feel-good' neurotransmitters. They enhance your mood immediately, making you feel happy from the inside.

What are three things you are grateful for?

316   Check out your feelings

The next time you start to feel lonely, mad, anxious, sad, scared or jealous, pause for a moment. Notice how you were about to respond. Were you were about to grab your phone to scroll through Instagram or check your email? Resist the urge and, instead, sit down or lay down (face down is better) and close your eyes. See if you can locate a physical sensation in your body. Do you feel a tightness in your chest? In your gut? Butterflies in your chest? Tightness in your throat? Is your jaw clenched? Whatever sensation you find, really go into that sensation. Forget the thoughts swirling around and don't try to figure out what emotions you're having if they are unclear. Just go into the physical sensation and really feel it. Stay with the physical feeling for a few minutes. Then ask it what it's trying to tell you.

The technique has been used in ancient yogic practices. You'll be surprised how much insight you get from this, and you'll probably prevent yourself from doing the harming habit that you usually resort to to ignore your feelings. Sitting with your emotions may be one of the most difficult things you'll ever do, but it will improve your relationships, help heal old traumas, allow you to break free of bad habits and get you to your next level of personal development.

317   The power of resilience

Most of us have grown up with the bedtime story of the hare and the tortoise – if not, refresh your memory by looking at idea 151. The tortoise was the hero because being 'slow and steady' won the race. Take a moment more and remind yourself of the stories of Neil Armstrong, Isaac Newton, Thomas Edison, Dr Shirley Jackson, Marie Curie and Grace Hopper. These were people who believed in an unseen reality but kept moving forward without being bogged down by failure, adversity or barriers. Edison got the light bulb right after thousands of failed attempts!

If you can recognise and leverage the power of resilience, you can find opportunities in every adversity and still thrive. Your self-perceptions are influenced by your cognitive biases and so you might underestimate yourself. You may find yourself focusing on roadblocks more than your goals and this can often lead to frustration, agony and hopelessness. Practising resilience helps you to bounce back each time you get derailed.

318   Know yourself

Your resilience is your ability to bounce back from tough times and difficulties. But resilience is not a trampoline, where you're down one moment and up the next. It's more like climbing a mountain without a map – it takes time, strength and help from people around you.

A great step to increase your resilience is to develop self-awareness. Self-awareness is having a clear perception of your own personality. Make a list of your strengths, weaknesses, thoughts, beliefs, motivation, emotions. This awareness allows you to understand how other people perceive you, your attitude and your responses to them in the moment.

319   Challenge yourself

Create an environment every day where 'the challenge exceeds your skill'. Challenge yourself daily to perform in some way beyond where your existing skills lie. By doing this, you create a gap between where you're currently at and the skills you need to develop in order to accomplish a certain task or challenge. This gap is your opportunity for growth. Creating an environment where the challenge exceeds your skill means you'll be developing your mental toughness daily.

320   Maximise your motivation

If you're finding something too easy, it can kill your motivation because it doesn't present a challenge and take you out of your comfort zone. Challenge can be defined as the amount of mental effort that you must exert to perform an activity. Create a challenge to get you out of your comfort zone, so that your capabilities will be stretched, your motivation maximised and your enthusiasm and interest engaged. It is the difficult and seemingly impossible things that will really develop you and spur you on to spectacular, greater achievements.

321   Careful what you think

If you truly want to change what you are doing and how you are behaving, you must first alter your thoughts. If your thoughts created undesirable behaviour, they may be negative thoughts from early childhood, or thoughts that you've loaded into your mind through negative self-talk. Your negative self-talk may come from you directly, or from your interpretation of what you hear other people say to you or about you. But beware, your negative self-talk will become negative thinking and turn into negative behaviour. Thankfully, your positive self-talk will become positive thinking and positive behaviour. Be careful about what you think!

322   Burn your boats

In 1519 Spanish conquistador Hernán Cortés, while attempting to conquer the Aztec empire, burned his ships after landing in Mexico. He knew his men would fight harder if he removed all possibility of retreat.

When you commit 100 per cent, you're burning your boats, too. See your goals through to completion. Let that be your only choice.

323   Build your mental muscle

Building mental toughness is fundamental to being able to live your best life. Just as you go to the gym and lift weights in order to build your physical muscles, you must also develop your mental health and toughness through the use of mental tools and techniques. You're able to become mentally stronger – the key is to keep practising and exercising your mental muscles, just as you would if you were trying to build physical strength.

Start to build your mental muscle today by doing one difficult thing you've been avoiding. Consciously challenge yourself to do something today that sits just outside your comfort zone. Do it again tomorrow and the next day. Very soon you will realise that you're building mental muscle, and the ability to achieve more than you thought you could.

324   Create a not-to-do list

Do you get easily distracted? It can take up to 25 minutes to regain your focus after being distracted. The good news is, you can learn to refocus by building your 'attention muscle' and the first step is to create a 'not-to-do list'.

Whenever you feel the pull to check Facebook or follow any other random thought that comes into your head, write it down instead. The act of simply transferring that thought from mind to paper allows you to stay focused on the task at hand. You can also train your attentional muscle with games like chess, sudoku and memory games.

325   Breathe it out

Whether it's as part of formal meditation or on an as-needed basis, deep breathing is essential for developing your mental toughness. It allows you to better regulate your thoughts, feelings and, well, breathing when the going gets rough. Deep breathing helps reduce cortisol levels in the brain and body that are blocking your cognition, allowing you to decompress. Hyperventilating can make you feel worse, while deep slow breathing calms you down, reducing your adrenaline and cortisol. It helps your stress reaction to work for you and not against you, preparing you for positive action.

Try these two breathing techniques:

- The 10-second pause is where you breathe in for three seconds and out for seven seconds.
- The box breathing method is where you breathe in deeply for four seconds, hold for four seconds and breathe out for four seconds. You can also breathe in one side of your nose and out the other side.

The oxygen flow from deep breathing helps reset the deepest parts of your brain and biochemistry.

326   Break the cycle

When bad things happen, you may get stuck thinking about negative outcomes. You might repeatedly think about what you could have done differently in the past, or how you're going to mess up again in the future. You ruminate on these events because you mistakenly believe that thinking about your hardships over and over again will help you solve them. Unfortunately, negative thought cycles just get you caught up in your thoughts instead of taking the actions you need to move forward.

To put an end to these negative thought cycles, which have become well-worn pathways in our brains, you need to short-circuit your thoughts mid-cycle. To do this, create an action plan for what you'll do when your negative thought cycles get going. So instead of trying to think your way out of your emotions, drop everything and do something different – go for a run or change your location. This break forces your brain and your body to completely switch gears and focus on something else entirely, thus breaking the negative thought cycle.

327   Break it down

With everything you have going on, it can be hard to stay focused on your long-term goals, especially when you don't see immediate or quick results. Keep your attention on the long-term outcomes to stay steady in the face of real (or potential) obstacles.

When you are working on a large goal, breaking it down into small bite-size pieces will help you stay consistent. This will give you something to work on and to achieve every day. The smaller, manageable goals will give you regular little wins. Those little wins will provide the motivation you need to keep going and stay focused on the long-term goals.

Write down your long-term goal and then draw a mind map of all the smaller goals you'll need to achieve along the way.

328   Confidence on the rise

On your journey to develop your mental toughness, your sense of control will rise. Control of your life and control of your emotions. The more control you feel you possess, the more confidence you'll have to overcome obstacles and resolve complications.

When you haven't mastered something relevant to achieving your goal, you give yourself the impression that you lack control. This impression may cause you to feel unprepared, lacking in the skills to achieve success, and you may become more inclined to give up when you face adversity.

Mastery is essential for developing mental toughness. When you're proficient in something, you trust yourself. You have confidence in your skill and abilities. This confidence reinforces your resilience and makes you more likely to press on than surrender to defeat.

329   Bounce back

You weren't born knowing how to recover from setbacks, it's not intuitive – it's something you learn. You'll already have discovered, from various experiences, that failures are seldom disastrous or final. When you stumble, you can pick yourself up, dust yourself off and carry on. The more often you bounce back, the easier it becomes.

The key to quickly recovering from setbacks is twofold. First, immediately confront your negative thoughts regarding the setback and acknowledge what you're thinking. Second, re-engage your mind that recognises your abilities, creativity and self-worth. The more you practise recovering from setbacks, the more motivated you'll feel, and you'll soon find you are dusting yourself off and bouncing back instinctively.

330   Bored?

What feelings do you typically associate with boredom? Some may be negative but there'll probably be some positives in there, too. Things like restlessness, frustration, calmness, satisfaction, irritability, amusement, guilt, optimism or pessimism.

Now, reframe those negative emotions. So if, for example, you typically feel restless when you're bored, determine the reason. Perhaps you were raised to believe that idle time is worthless and you should always be doing something. In this case you can reframe the idle time as valuable downtime during which you have an opportunity to relax and recharge.

CHAPTER 12

BE READY FOR CHANGE

331   The story of two grains

Two grains were lying side by side on the fertile soil. The first grain said, 'I want to grow up. I want to put down roots deep into the ground and sprout from the ground. I dream of blossoming in delicate buds and proclaim the coming of spring. I want to feel the warm rays of sun and the dew drops on my petals.' This grain grew up and became a beautiful flower.

The second grain said, 'I'm afraid. If I put down my roots into the ground, I don't know what they will face there. If I grow tender stems, they can be damaged by wind. If I grow flowers, they may be disrupted. So I'd rather wait for a safer time.' So the second grain waited, until a chicken passed by and pecked it up.

The Lesson: If you have a dream, do something with it. The first small step you take will make a great difference. If you just wait for perfect conditions and keep worrying about what obstacles you may face, you'll end up doing nothing and your dream will die. Don't kill your dream – believe in yourself and take your very first step, even if it's a tiny little step.

332   Beware the lazy beast

There is nothing wrong with taking the opportunity to relax, or even feeling a little lazy. The alternative to listening to your body telling you when you need to rest is burnout, and burnout is a much greater threat to your performance and productivity than bouts of laziness.

Having said that, laziness can breed additional laziness if it's left unchecked. Suppose your alarm goes off in the morning and rather than immediately getting out of bed you hit the snooze button. After a few minutes you hit it again. And then again. By the time you finally get out of bed you're feeling sluggish and you're now running late. Your morning is off to an idle start and that sets the tone for your performance for the rest of the day.

Laziness can open the door to a sense of lethargy, and that feeling of sluggishness will make you less likely to persevere when things go wrong rather than digging in and persisting.

333   Bendy, flexible thinking

If change is truly the only constant, then flexibility and adaptability are among the most important traits you can develop. If you become a flexible thinker, you'll be able to consider a range of possible consequences of your actions rather than only considering an optimistic view, or only considering a pessimistic view.

It's important that you don't assume that your way of looking at something is the way everyone looks at it. When you can see that other people look at situations in different ways, it will help you not jump to inaccurate conclusions and to make better decisions. Really flexible thinkers can adjust their general tendency to be positive or negative based on which is more helpful in a given situation. Flexible thinkers don't assume that how they feel now is how they're always going to feel.

When you're next in a situation where you feel intimidated, recognise that you're likely to feel more confident over time, as you gain more experience with this kind of issue.

334   Accept your lot

Acceptance can be a confusing concept. Why should you accept things that might be considered 'unacceptable' or 'bad'? Start to look at the idea of accepting things the way they are, as your ability to develop a more positive attitude towards something, even when it isn't good for you or ethically acceptable to you.

It's entirely normal to find acceptance a challenging concept, so allow yourself to feel the way you do and relax about it. Try to visualise what acceptance would look like, how you would feel and behave if you could accept this thing the way it is. Be kind, patient and understanding of yourself – you will eventually see things differently and be calmer about everything.

335 Believe in yourself before anything else

When you truly believe in yourself, you will be unstoppable. Once you solidify your belief in yourself, success is 100 per cent possible for you. When you struggle with your confidence, you'll tend to focus on things you can't do. That's because you feel weaknesses more acutely. When you fail over and over at something that seems easy to others, it's nearly impossible to believe in yourself.

Deliberately practise whatever you need to do to achieve your goals and you will see huge improvements quickly. Your self-confidence will grow and you'll also be more able to manage and inspire others with assurance and direction.

336 Be thankful

I want to encourage you to develop an 'attitude of gratitude'. Gratitude is the quality of being thankful, the readiness you have to show appreciation and to return kindness. When you can develop more gratitude in your life, you'll start to unlock a great deal of power to create happiness. Power to see the goodness in your life, build meaningful relationships and relish great experiences.

Don't waste time being envious of anyone else's car, house, spouse, job or family. Instead, be grateful for what you have. Focus on what you've achieved and what you're going to achieve, instead of looking over your shoulder and being envious of what someone else has.

What can you be grateful for today? Who can you show kindness to today?

337   Bees shouldn't fly

It's aerodynamically impossible for the bumblebee to fly as its wings are too short and its body weight is too high. However, nobody has told this to the bumblebee and so it just goes on flying. Great things are often achieved by people who are unaware of their limitations or just don't accept them.

You are primarily responsible for where you are right now in life, and for your own destiny. Some people go through life blaming their parents, teachers, circumstances, luck and other people for their lack of success. Some people blame their lack of formal education and their upbringing for holding them back, but we all know people with little formal education and/or from disadvantaged backgrounds who have gone on to become highly successful through persistence, hard work, dedication and determination.

Attributing blame to others for your circumstances does not lead to empowerment, responsibility or control over your life and behaviour. Instead, take action right now to change the direction of your life in a positive way. Learn from your mistakes. View failure as a learning experience on the road to achieving your ultimate goal. There is no failure, only feedback.

338   Be your own special guest

Treat yourself as well as you would a special guest. You're not the only one who would do anything for someone else, but when it comes to yourself, it's sometimes tough to even muster an 'I like you'. The absolute truth is that the way you treat yourself, the way you treat others and the way they treat you are all connected.

To help you to treat yourself better you must start by loving and appreciating yourself. Think of yourself, your feelings and your thoughts as being like plants – either weeds or flowers; it's you who gets to water the ones you want to see thrive. If you asked a friend what they thought of you, what might they say? What would they say your strengths are? What do they love most about you? Ask them and start to love yourself a little bit more.

339   Be specific

Make your goal really specific. Vague goals are practically useless. Don't set goals like 'I want to run faster', 'I want to lose weight', 'I want to be rich' because they have no definition to them. Specifics ensure that your goals are performance based rather than outcome based. Specifics guarantee feedback so that you can adjust the goal, if needed. Ensure you have as much control over your goals as possible.

Importantly, any goal should improve or change your behaviour because its intent is to make you better. Effective goals need to be positive, precise and written down. I can almost 100 per cent assure you that, if you do this, you will be more successful.

340   Ask yourself

Take a moment to check in with yourself about your mood so that you can begin to gain some control of your emotions. Ask yourself: 'What am I feeling right now? What happened to make me feel this way? Does the situation have a different explanation that might make sense? What do I want to do about these feelings? Is there a better way of coping with them?'

By considering possible alternatives, you'll be reframing your thoughts, which will help you to modify extreme reactions. It can take some time before this response becomes a habit, but, with practice, going through these steps in your head will become easier every day.

341   Be proactive

A big part of building mental toughness is gaining emotional control, and this takes time. You may be heavily influenced by your emotions, even the ones that are unreasonable, given your abilities. So it will inevitably take time to learn how to manage them.

Scrutinise negative emotions the moment they surface and ask yourself, 'Are these emotions reasonable?' Reflect on how these emotions may be holding you back.

Meditate for five minutes a day in order to observe your emotions without judgement. Get accustomed to letting go of your frustrations and start to take action even when you're uncertain of the outcome. This will train your mind to be proactive.

342   Be present

It's best for you to invest your time and energy in developing skills to recognise and minimise negative self-talk rather than spending the time trying to overcome them once they've occurred. If you replace negative self-talk with positive self-talk, you'll notice the difference in your sense of wellbeing immediately.

You'll eliminate the type of thinking that limits your behaviour and capability. You'll be consciously thinking in the present. Positive change can be made in the present and high achievers are people who spend their time there. Those who spend more time in the past or the future are usually worriers.

343   Anywhere, anytime

Practise some simple meditation today. I'm not talking about sitting with crystals, uttering mantras or strengthening your root chakra. I mean sit for a few minutes with your eyes closed and focus on your breathing. Simply be present in the moment. Notice the sound of your breathing and relax every muscle in your body.

This simple meditation allows you to disconnect from the world, giving you a brief respite from all its deadlines, expectations and stresses. It gives you a chance to catch your breath.

Science tells us that meditation triggers activity in the anterior cingulate cortex (ACC), the area of your brain that contributes to attention regulation, decision making, impulse control and emotional responses.

You can practise simple meditation anywhere and at any time. All you need is a bit of quiet, a bit of privacy and five minutes.

344   Be fully committed

You have set yourself a goal or task. It could be anything, big or small, from giving up caffeine to going to the gym every day or preparing a presentation. In order to complete this task you need to be fully committed. I have always seen commitment as all or nothing – on or off. When you commit to something 50 per cent, you are not committed – you are simply having a go. And just having a go is nothing like a commitment. There are no degrees of commitment – you are either committed or not.

Anything less than 100 per cent commitment puts you in a danger zone where you can easily talk yourself out of anything, give yourself excuses and allow yourself the 'get-out' you are secretly hoping for. Commit to your task 100 per cent, with no ifs, buts, excuses or get-outs.

What will you commit to today, 100 per cent?

345   Be decisive

If you have ambitious goals, then a lot of effort will be required to reach them. You'll need to develop the ability to make decisions and stick by them. You'll need to make strong, specific decisions so that you can become more determined. Your decision will indicate your direction. It shows you how to move forward even when you begin to encounter challenges or setbacks on your path.

Your decisions will be set in stone, which in turn will motivate you through hard times and keep you focused during easier times. Your determination begins with deciding what you want and sticking to your decision no matter what.

346   Get what you deserve

Your unconscious will allow you to have only what you believe you deserve. The more you hang on to any negativity about yourself, the less you'll think you deserve. If you have a small view of yourself, then you'll feel as if you deserve poverty. Your subconscious will keep you stuck.

Your subconscious, and your personality, are your comfort zone. Stepping outside of your comfort zone creates feelings of uncertainty and often fear, but you can shatter your subconscious limitations by taking bold actions towards your future self. Telling people about your goals can make a powerful impression on your subconscious, but you'll need to take action. Taking action will give you satisfaction as you move towards your goal.

347   Be careful what you focus on

However good or bad a situation is now, it will change. Nothing lasts for ever. Things will change and brightness will return to your life. Don't waste your energy on things that you cannot control, but instead focus on things that are within your reach.

One thing you can always control is yourself and how you respond to situations. Some of the things you cannot influence will set the context for what you can influence. Be aware of them, but don't focus on them. When you focus on the things that are within your influence and pour your energy into them, it's much more likely you'll achieve your desired outcome.

Focus only on what you can influence or control.

348   Seek change

Mental toughness requires that you be flexible to your circumstances when things go wrong. You need to be able to adapt in order to act with purpose. Most of us dread change. We enjoy predictability because it reduces uncertainty. Fear of uncertainty is one of the biggest obstacles to taking purposeful action. Building the habit of flexible thinking requires you to leave your comfort zone. It calls for you to actively seek changes that you can incorporate into your life.

The upside is that doing so desensitises you to change in circumstances, increasing your tolerance of them. And as your tolerance increases, your fear will naturally erode.

349   Be prepared

To manage any fear or anxiety you are feeling, have a plan – be prepared – because you will then have a process to work through, whenever you need it. Even if the worst happens, with a plan in place you will be prepared to handle your fears, even if they turn into reality. This applies to your personal life and your professional life

Identify something specific you want to do but about which you have some fear or trepidation. Draw three columns on a piece of paper:

In column 1, list your specific fear – what you are most worried about happening.

In column 2, list all the things you could do to reduce the chance of this happening or its impact if it does happen.

In column 3, make a list of the worst that could happen if your fear were to become a reality.

Then, importantly, ask yourself: What is the cost of doing nothing? Or not doing the thing you want to do?

Make a plan. Be prepared. And see what happens when you decide to take action on that plan.

350   Anxiety is normal

Anxiety is defined as a pervasive feeling of unease, worry or fear which ranges from a mild level to more acute levels of severity. Anxiety is part and parcel of the human condition. It relates to situations you perceive as threatening, uncontrollable or unavoidable. We all get stressed and we all get anxious, but things can become problematic if you aren't managing the feelings well and you start to feel continuously worried and anxious.

You can reduce feelings of anxiety immediately by taking a walk outside in the fresh air, taking 10 minutes to meditate or taking several deep breaths, exhaling and inhaling slowly.

351   And breathe…

Deep breathing exercises can be a really effective way to break negative thought cycles. Excuse yourself for five minutes to practise deep, slow breathing.

Deep breathing helps activate your parasympathetic nervous system, which can both calm you and switch off your stress. When you're learning this strategy, it can be helpful to use it often, even if you're only a little worked up. This can make it easier to implement in more challenging situations.

Try it a few times to start short-circuiting your negative emotional cycles, helping you to recover from challenges more easily.

352   An attitude of gratitude

Much like seeing physical gains from working out and eating more healthily, you can develop healthy mental toughness habits, like practising gratitude. Take time to notice and reflect upon the things that you're thankful for. You'll experience more positive emotions, feel more alive, sleep better, express more compassion and kindness, and even build a stronger immune system.

The best way to reap the benefits of gratitude is to notice new things you're grateful for every day. So start to keep a gratitude journal. At the beginning or end of each day, write down three things you are grateful for and why. At the end of each week, read through your journal to remind yourself of all the things you feel grateful for. Keeping your gratitude journal will slowly change the way you perceive situations by adjusting what you focus on.

353   Get out of your head

To improve the life you are living in your head, you will have to take action in the external world. You can become trapped inside your head, torturing yourself by overthinking, ruminating over unhelpful thoughts. This will need to stop if your life is going to improve and you are going to find happiness.

Your real and exciting life will always exist outside your mind.

You have to take action. Any action. Get out of your head and into the world.

Do something today which you takes you forward. New actions require effort, so today do the most important thing that deep down, you know will help you. Do it.

354   Actively listen

If there's one place your limited attention span is incredibly noticeable, it's when you're talking to others. Instead of letting your mind wander during a conversation, practise attentive listening by not interrupting, recapping what the other person has said regularly, and using connecting words like 'OK', 'I get it' and 'Yes' to stay engaged and show that you're listening.

These active listening skills not only help you come across as a nicer, more interesting person, they also help train your mind to focus on the person in front of you.

355   A mouldy take

If it weren't for a small mistake made by Scottish scientist Alexander Fleming in 1928, the past 90 years could have looked very different. Fleming discovered the antibiotic penicillin after a petri dish he had left out while on holiday became contaminated with a *Penicillium* mould. He noticed that where the mould grew, bacteria didn't, and this led to the development and production of penicillin.

Since then, the infection-fighting drug has helped save millions of lives. Mistakes can often offer opportunity.

356 Action!

It is important for you to commit to taking action. You need to fully understand your circumstances before responding to them, of course, and that requires reflection and contemplation, but eventually you must act.

Even though life is unpredictable and the outcome of your actions and decisions will always be uncertain, you must adopt an action mindset. This mindset instils courage and enables you to confront challenges without being paralysed by your limitations.

357 Accept it has happened

Accept that it has happened. The only way out is through, and to get through anything you must first accept the truth. Don't ignore it or pretend it didn't happen; just know that setbacks are a natural part of life. Accepting it will help you overcome it and get you back on the right path. No one gets anywhere by not acknowledging that they've experienced hardship. There is power in acceptance of what's happened, so stop resisting the reality and find the lesson.

358 A smile is worth a thousand words

You can get through challenges and setbacks and come out even stronger when you can quickly and easily build rapport with people. When you need to build rapport, make sure your words and body language are aligned and that both are non-threatening. A simple smile is the most powerful non-verbal technique you can use to appear accommodating and friendly. Speak slowly as quick speech can sound nervous and jumpy, not confident. Crazy people tend to speak quickly, whereas self-assured people speak slowly.

Today, practise building rapport by smiling and speaking more slowly and notice what happens!

359   A plan for managing emotion

When you are in the eye of the storm of a setback or adversity, you can learn to hold your emotional reactions in order to make better decisions. In the process of 'holding your emotional reaction' you give yourself a chance to tap into some objectivity or a new perspective which will help you to establish what action/reaction is necessary to reach the outcome you desire or require. Failure is sometimes exactly what you need, in order to know what strategies you're missing.

The more efficient your basic strategies and procedures are, the easier it is to remain mentally tough because it is the stability of those procedures that gives you something to count on and hold on to. Intense emotions aren't all bad – emotions and strong feelings make your life exciting. And it's perfectly normal to experience occasional emotional overwhelm – when something wonderful happens, when something terrible happens, when you feel like you've missed out.

You can't control your emotions with a dial, but you can start to control them by having strategies and plans lined up for when you need them.

360   A long-term view

Have you got a long-term goal in mind? Regular evaluation of this goal will help you determine whether you have set realistic expectations. One of the fastest ways to become discouraged in pursuit of your goal is if it is unrealistic or unattainable. To avoid discouragement and feelings of defeat, you need to be realistic in your expectations.

Evaluate the progress you've made towards your goal at the end of each week and you'll easily determine what will best help you achieve your ultimate goal. As you build on your smaller goals, you get closer to achieving your larger goal and maintain the motivation and momentum to keep going.

Write down your long-term goal and put it on a wall so you see it every day!

CHAPTER 13
LET GO OF YOUR FAILURES

361   The story of a carrot, an egg and a cup of coffee

A young woman talked to her mother about her life and how things were so hard for her. She didn't know how she was going to make it through and wanted to give up. She was tired of fighting and struggling. It seemed that as one problem was solved, a new one arose.

Her mother took her to the kitchen. She filled three pots with water and placed each on the hob. Soon the pots came to a boil. In the first she placed carrots, in the second she placed eggs and in the last she placed ground coffee beans. She let them sit and boil, without saying a word. In about 20 minutes she turned off the hob. She fished the carrots out and placed them in a bowl. She pulled the eggs out and placed them in a bowl. Then she ladled the coffee out and placed it in a bowl.

Turning to her daughter, she asked, 'Tell me, what do you see?' 'Carrots, eggs and coffee,' the daughter replied. Her mother brought her closer and asked her to feel the carrots. She did and noted that they were soft. The mother then asked the daughter to take an egg and break it. After pulling off the shell, she observed the hard-boiled egg. Finally, the mother asked the daughter to sip the coffee. The daughter smiled as she tasted its rich aroma.

The daughter then asked, 'What does it mean, Mother?' Her mother explained that each of these objects had faced the same adversity – boiling water. Each reacted differently. The carrot went in strong, hard and unrelenting. However, after being subjected to the boiling water, it softened and became weak. The egg had been fragile. Its thin outer shell had protected its liquid interior, but after sitting in the boiling water, its insides became hardened. The ground coffee beans were unique, however. After they were in the boiling water, they had changed the water.

The Lesson: When adversity knocks on your door, how do you respond? Are you a carrot, an egg or a coffee bean? The happiest people don't necessarily have the best of everything, they just make the most of everything that comes their way. The brightest future will always be based on a forgotten past. You can't go forward in life until you let go of your past failures and heartaches.

362   A bit of gardening

Imagine your mind as a plot of garden, where the soil is rich and ready for planting. Imagine that, each time you have a negative thought, you are planting a weed into that soil. Each time you have a positive thought, you're planting a flower. At the end of the day, step back and see whether you have a group of weeds, a beautiful flower garden or a mixture.

If you have an abundance of flowers, you've been planting positive thoughts and you'll be feeling happy and uplifted. If you see an overgrown area of weeds, you can be assured that you've been sowing negative thoughts and may be feeling sad or depressed and displaying negative behaviour.

Be sure, every day, to plant flowers, not weeds. Doing something for one day, or for just a few days, will not bring any significant or serious changes to your life. Your success will happen as a result of making continuous changes. It's a process.

If you want to replace your bad habits with good ones, you'll need to take action daily – only then will you make space for that particular change. For example, if you want to stay fit, then one day of taking exercise will not help – you need to exercise daily if you want to see and feel evidence of an improvement.

363   On reflection

What have you learned about yourself in the past 12 months? Write down 10 ways you have grown personally or professionally in the past year.

Think about specific skills you have improved, such as giving/receiving feedback, managing your time or seeing setbacks as opportunities to learn and grow. Maybe you have become more patient or compassionate.

Read over your list and notice your internal state. Feeling proud, strong or even relief from negative self-talk means your brain is getting more resilient. Read over the list frequently until you internalise these wonderful accomplishments. Your self-talk will improve a bit with each reading. That shift in thinking will grow your true confidence.

364   2000-year-old truths

Epictetus was a Greek philosopher who was known for his influence on the doctrines of Stoicism, a philosophy that taught mental toughness. His wise words are as true today as they were 2000 years ago:

'When you are offended at any man's fault, turn to yourself and study your own failings. Then you will forget your anger.'

'Decide to be extraordinary and do what you need to do – now.'

'No matter what happens, it is within my power to turn it to my advantage.'

'Any person capable of angering you becomes your master.'

'Freedom is the only worthy goal in life. It is won by disregarding things that lie beyond our control.'

365   Moving on

You may be suffering from a loss or heartbreak right now. Remember that your mental health and mental toughness will never improve or develop if you continue to search for happiness in the same negative, toxic places that you lost it.

The people who have been negative or destructive in your life will remain that way. That job is still boring. That person is still an idiot. That relationship is still toxic.

Remember that your past is your past. You have to look forward, to move forward.

Take action today to move away from those negative experiences and towards exciting new opportunities.

CONCLUSION

Every one of us encounters setbacks and misfortune; it's an inevitability. What really matters, though, is how you respond to those setbacks. I hope that, with the help of the tips in this book, you can always find something to lift you, help you progress and keep you determined.

You are way stronger than you think. You have far more resource than you can imagine and it would be a tragedy if you didn't tap into that resource and discover how amazing you are!

What a waste it would be if you took all your potential to your grave. Are you ready to get out of your comfort zone and take some risks and do some things you have never done before?

IT'S TIME TO SEIZE THE DAY.
ALL 365 OF THEM.

365 – your day-by-day guide to living better and working smarter

365 Ways to be More Stoic 978-1-52939-044-5

365 Ways to Develop Mental Toughness 978-1-52939-764-2

365 Ways to Save the Planet 978-1-52939-741-3

365 Ways to Live Mindfully 978-1-52939-039-1

365 Ways to Have a Good Day 978-1-52938-224-2

365 WAYS TO HAVE A GOOD DAY

By Ian Sanders

365 WAYS TO HAVE A GOOD DAY is a full year's worth of daily inspiration, tools, habits, actions, and rituals that will help you live your best life. You'll discover surprising insights from psychologists, business leaders, entrepreneurs and designers. You'll explore the benefits of Feierabends and Laughies, have your eyes opened by a dance psychologist, and find out why one senior executive's tattooed fingers help him make the right career choices.

"An inspiring, heart-warming, go-getting book ... an antidote to apathy."

Helen Tupper, co-author of *The Squiggly Career*

Hardback 978-1-52938-224-2

272pp 198×129mm

365 WAYS TO BE MORE STOIC

By Tim Lebon with Kasey Pierce

365 WAYS TO BE MORE STOIC is a full year's worth of daily inspiration, tools, stories, actions, and rituals that will guide you to a meaningful life, filled with happiness. You'll learn to navigate through the controllable and inevitable. You'll develop constructive ways to handle frustration, adversity and even your own mortality. You'll learn habit-forming strategies, pick up helpful concepts, and uncover tips for lasting change.

Hardback 978-1-52939-044-5

288pp 198×129mm

365 WAYS TO LIVE MINDFULLY

By Pascale Engelmajer

365 WAYS TO LIVE MINDFULLY contains a full year's worth of daily inspiration, stories, practices, exercises and meditations that will help you live more mindfully. You'll learn ways to focus your attention on your present experience, to be fully in the moment, and to create a life that's consistent with your values and aspirations. You'll develop habit-forming strategies, pick up helpful concepts, and discover tips for lasting change.

Hardback 978-1-52939-039-1

240pp 198×129mm